LIGHT FROM BIBLE PROPHECY

LIGHT FROM BIBLE PROPHECY

As Related to the Present Crisis

By
LOUIS S. BAUMAN, D.D.

INTRODUCTION BY
CHARLES G. TRUMBULL, Litt.D.
Editor, The Sunday School Times

NEW YORK
Fleming H. Revell Company
LONDON AND EDINBURGH

1940

Printed in the United States of America

New York: 158 Fifth Avenue
London: 21 Paternoster Square

To my beloved son

PAUL R. BAUMAN

of Los Angeles, California

I dedicate this book, with the prayer that, should the Lord, before His appearing, call me home by way of the valley, this ministry of holding aloft God's Light for man's night, shall be perpetuated by my son, until the Lord, Whom having not seen, we both love, shall come

Louis D. Bauman

AUTHOR'S NOTE

THE reader is requested to bear in mind, as he peruses the pages of this book, that this book contains a series of articles written for the *Sunday School Times* over a period of one year, and without thought of their publication in a single volume. Great changes took place in the political world within that year. The nations of Europe were overrun by the German dictator, Adolf Hitler. France fell an easy prey to German and Italian power, and is in a state of complete collapse. Italy entered the war on the side of Germany.

These articles were written to deal with *current events* in the light of divine revelation. Naturally, as the scene shifted from time to time, it was necessary to repeat what had been aforetime written, in order to deal with those events. This brought the subject of the Roman Empire frequently into discussion, for the Roman Empire in its final form must occupy the center of the stage as the sun of Gentile dominion sinks low in the West to rise no more. With the passing of that Empire the Kingdom of God will come to earth and "the Son of righteousness" shall arise "with healing in His wings" over all the earth, and "sorrow and sighing shall flee away."

L. S. B.

Long Beach, Calif.

INTRODUCTION

NEXT to a saving knowledge of the Lord Jesus Christ as
one's personal Savior, a knowledge of God's prophetic
program for the age in which we are living, and for the age
to come, is of supreme importance—more vitally important
now than in any earlier centuries. The world is being shaken
to its foundations, civilization is tottering, "men's hearts failing them for fear, and for looking after those things which
are coming on the earth," as the fresh and unprecedented
tragedies of such wars as the world has never before known are
destroying the lives of nations and breaking human hearts
throughout the world. Those who do not know Bible Prophecy
cannot understand or interpret the events that are crowding
our daily papers and filling our ears with their cabled and
radioed reports. Hence Christian people who have not been
prepared for the epoch in which we are now living are bewil-
dered, terrified, and well-nigh losing their Christian faith.

These undeniable facts give Dr. Bauman's new volume a
priceless value to our generation. When, in September of
1939, I was led to ask this outstanding student and teacher of
Bible Prophecy to write seven articles for *The Sunday School
Times* on Bible Prophecy in relation to the European War,
neither he nor I had any thought that the proposed modest
series of seven would grow until it became twenty-five illumi-
nating articles. The War has grown until it threatens the
whole world, and many and urgent have been the requests
from Christian people for Dr. Bauman's entire series in permanent form. I rejoice that these invaluable contributions have
been brought together in the present volume, for it is a book
that Christian people and all others who would be intelligently
informed of the meaning of the events in the midst of which
we are living should read, and circulate as widely as possible
among their friends.

I am convinced that Dr. Bauman's studies as given in this

volume make one of the most valuable series of interpretations of Bible Prophecy that have been published in our generation. With lucid clearness, inviting simplicity, Scriptural faithfulness, and a brilliant literary style, this profound student of the Word and of current events has made a rich and classic contribution to our understanding of the "more sure word of prophecy" which is God's gift as "a light that shineth in a dark place" (2 Pet. 1:19).

CHARLES G. TRUMBULL.

Philadelphia, Pa.

CONTENTS

CONTENTS

IX. The "Beasts" and the World's Greatest Massacre (*Cont.*)

the "red horse"? Is Mussolini possibly the rider of the "white horse"? The present war the world's "greatest massacre." World dictators, "beasts" in the form of men. Man's boasted advancement, an illusion. Hoover prophesies world famine. "The stuff of Paradise" that failed. The beastly nature of Stalin. Germany's degenerate rulers. "The darkest hour in the world's history," pregnant with hope.

X. "And There Shall Be Earthquakes" . . .   73

Nature responds to the perfect will of God. A pre-Adamic world and its judgment. Sodom and Gomorrah. The plagues of Egypt. The earthquake in the days of Uzziah. "The earth did quake" at the crucifixion. Gibbon's declaration. The eruption of Mont Pelee. The destruction of Pompeii. The San Francisco earthquake. The destruction of Messina. The Japanese earthquake of 1923. The quakes in China. The recent Turkish quake, a judgment? Great earthquakes still to come. The significance of earthquakes. An incident in the Long Beach earthquake.

XI. Why the End of the Age Must Be Very Near   84

God keeps covenant. The promises of Christ cannot fail. The scoffer's sneer and Peter's warning.

XII. Signs of the End That Have Never Occurred Before   88

Signs that have never occurred before in answer to the scoffer's sneer:

A. *The synchronization of the greatest war, greatest famines, greatest pestilence, and greatest earthquakes of all time.* The World War, the greatest war. The world's greatest famines, in Russia and in China. The "flu" epidemic of 1918, the world's greatest pestilence. The earthquakes of Japan and China, the world's greatest quakes. "All these are the beginning of sorrows."

B. *Anti-Semitism engulfs the Jewish race.* Anti-Semitism world-wide.

march of the hosts of Antichrist. Rimming the Mediterranean. Dictators unconsciously fulfil the eternal purposes of God. The conquering Antichrist in Egypt. "The indignation." Antichrist at the zenith of his power. The three stepping stones of the Antichrist to power: (a) The "great whore"; or, ecclesiastical Rome; (b) Some great political power, probably Germany; (c) Jews, deceived by the false messiah. The "ten kings" who shall "have one mind." The "tidings" that "trouble" the Antichrist. The King of the North mobilizes and marches into Palestine. Antichrist, conqueror of Egypt, backward marches into Palestine. The great battle in Esdraelon, the doom of Gog. Antichrist rules the world. Antichrist deifies himself. Antichrist sets up his image in Jerusalem. The Jews refuse to worship his image. Antichrist, seeking the extermination of the Jews, commands an international army, and marches to the siege of Jerusalem.

Antichrist plants his palace on "the glorious holy mountain." "The siege against Judah and Jerusalem." Israel's last agony. "He shall be saved out of it." Every Jew in Jerusalem "shall be as David." He that is "Mighty to Save" rides forth from the open heavens, "the hope of His people" Israel, and the Savior of the world.

I

THE ROMAN EMPIRE MUST BE REVIVED

FUNDAMENTAL to an understanding of the prophetic message of the prophets of the living God, as that message concerns the Gentile powers of the earth, is a clear understanding of God's revelation of "the times of the Gentiles," which revelation was given to Nebuchadnezzar, through a dream. And, also, the revelation of the same "times," given to Daniel through "a dream and visions of his head upon his bed" (Dan. 7:1). The student of the prophetic word, endowed with a reasonable grasp of the message of God given to men in the two famous dreams recorded in Daniel, chapters 2 and 7, cannot go far astray in the entire field of prophetic revelation.

Therefore, as we approach the stage whereon the Gentile powers of the earth are even now enacting, as we believe, the final scenes of their awful tragedy, in a sincere effort to understand the meaning of it all, to answer, if it can be done, Daniel's query, "O my Lord, what shall be the end of these things?" (Dan. 12:8), we must stop and consider the divine interpretation of these two great dream-visions.

"The Times of the Gentiles."

The two dreams are one. Both are a revelation of "the times of the Gentiles"; that is, of the "times" (years) during which "Jerusalem shall be trodden down of the Gentiles" (Luke 21:24).

Those "times" began "with the overthrow of Zedekiah, in the year 586 B.C. [when] the kingdom of Judah was extinguished" (Ridpath). In that year, Nebuchadnezzar took Zedekiah off the throne, gouged out his eyes, provided him with bracelets in the form of chains, and carried him away to Babylon. Since that day, only one king *out of the loins of Jacob* has been crowned in Jerusalem, and He was crowned with thorns! Those

11

"times" will end when "the Stone of Israel" (Gen. 49:24) shall fall out of the heavens (Dan. 2:34) upon "the beast, and the kings of the earth, and their armies" (Rev. 19:19), and grind their bones to powder. Then the winds of earth, with a moan, will sweep their dust into eternal oblivion. And thus will pass the boasted power and vaunted glory of this present world!

The essential difference between the two dreams is, that to Nebuchadnezzar's human eyes, Gentile empire reared itself as a "great image, *whose brightness was excellent*" (Dan. 2:31); while, to Daniel's eyes, even as in God's eyes, Gentile empire appears as a den wherein "great beasts,"—rapacious, cruel, snarling, growling beasts, with bloody jaws foaming with hate and madness—rage in their lust and fury. As I write, these Gentile "beasts," living true to their characters, are tearing in pieces and gorging their bellies with the flesh of the aged and feeble, the blood of mothers, and the tender flesh of little babes blown by bombs from their cradles.

Nebuchadnezzar beheld a great image. The head was gold. To Nebuchadnezzar, Daniel said, "Thou art this head of gold" (Dan. 2:38). Daniel saw this same kingdom, Babylon, "like a lion" (Dan. 7:4). Daniel told the Babylonian monarch that the sun of Babylon was to set, and another world power was to rise in its place. Doubtless, the self-deified ruler didn't like that message. But God wrote it upon the wall. Babylon's sun sank, to rise no more.

The breast and arms of the image were of silver. That was Medo-Persia. Daniel saw this kingdom "like to a bear" (Dan. 7:5). This mighty state likewise was to pass. It did.

The belly and thighs of the image were of brass. That was Greece. That was Alexander the Great, claiming his paternity from Jupiter, weeping when yet scarcely more than a boy because there were no more worlds to conquer. Daniel saw this kingdom as a swift leopard, leaping as having wings, and devouring as it leaped. It also passed away.

The Fourth World Kingdom and Its "Ten Toes."

The legs and feet of the image were of iron. That was "the fourth kingdom . . . strong as iron . . . [which was to] break

in pieces . . . and bruise" (Dan. 2:40) all the kingdoms of
the earth. And Rome did. Let it be carefully noted, that
legs, feet, and toes of this image, *all* were component parts of
the "fourth kingdom"—*Rome*.

Later, Daniel saw this same mighty empire in another form
—a nameless monster, "dreadful and terrible, and strong exceedingly; . . . and *it had ten horns*" (Dan. 7:7). Then,
Daniel was told by the messenger from heaven that "the ten
horns *out of this kingdom* are ten kings that shall arise" (Dan.
7:24).

As the prophet was gazing with wonderment upon this
strange beast, meditating especially upon the ten horns, "behold, there came up among them another little horn" (Dan.
7:8). And he "beheld, and the same horn made war with the
saints, and prevailed against them; until the Ancient of days
came, and judgment was given unto the saints of the most
High; and the time came that the saints possessed the kingdom" (Dan. 7:21, 22).

Every description of this "little horn" fits into the details
of "the king [who] shall do according to his will" described by
Daniel in chapter 11, verse 36; and, "that man of sin" described by Paul in 2 Thessalonians 2:3, 4; and, the hydra-
headed "beast . . . up out of the sea" described by the Seer
of Patmos in Revelation 13:1-7. In all three pictures it is a
"beast" who has "a mouth speaking great things and blasphe-
mies," and who uses his mouth "in blasphemy against God";
who, in self-deification, "exalteth himself above all that is
called God"; to whom "power was given . . . over all kindreds,
and tongues, and nations"; to whom "it was given . . . to
make war with the saints, and to overcome them"; who "shall
plant the tabernacles of his palace between the seas in the
glorious holy mountain," even in Palestine; and, finally, who
"shall come to his end, and none shall help him" (Dan. 11:45);
"whom the Lord . . . shall destroy with the brightness of His
coming" (2 Thess. 2:8); who, when the rider of the great white
horse thunders forth out of the open heavens (Rev. 19:11),
shall be "taken, and . . . cast alive into a lake of fire" (Rev.
19:20).

By no manner of reasonable interpretation can these Scriptures be made to fit into the views of those who hold that these prophecies have been fulfilled, commonly known as the preterists. The "little horn," "the king [who] shall do according to his will," the "man of sin," and "the beast,"—*the Antichrist*—are one person. And this satanic superman will come to his end only when the armies of the earth, under his command, shall be destroyed by "the brightness of His [Christ's] coming"; when "the Ancient of days" shall come, and "the judgment shall sit . . . and the kingdom and dominion, and the greatness of the kingdom under the whole heaven, shall be given to the people of the saints of the most High, Whose kingdom is an everlasting kingdom, and all dominions shall serve and obey Him" (Dan. 7:26, 27).

Surely, surely, with His saints, Christ does not yet reign! Not yet do "all dominions . . . serve and obey Him"! No, not *yet*—not while the blood-soaked, foamy-jawed brutes continue rampant over the world!

It is exceedingly important now to note that it was upon the feet and the toes of the image that Nebuchadnezzar saw the "stone [that] was cut out without hands" come crashing down. *Bear in mind the fact that those feet and toes were integral parts of that "fourth kingdom." They represented the Roman Empire in its final form.* No true interpretation can separate them from that dominion. *The Roman Empire, therefore, must be in existence when the "Stone" falls*—when the "KING OF KINGS, AND LORD OF LORDS" (Rev. 19:16) shall ride forth from His present seat of honor at the right hand of God, to establish the Kingdom of Heaven upon the earth. For, it is written:

"This man, after He had offered one sacrifice for sins for ever, sat down on the right hand of God; from henceforth expecting till His enemies be made His footstool" (Heb. 10:12, 13).

He shall not expect in vain!

Moreover, note that "the ten horns" that "are ten kings that shall arise," are "OUT OF THIS KINGDOM" (Dan. 7:24).

Beyond all cavil, "the ten horns" that "are ten kings" seen in Daniel's vision are the same "ten horns which . . . are ten kings" seen in John's vision (Rev. 17:12-17).

The only logical conclusion to which we can come is that the "ten toes" of Nebuchadnezzar's vision, belonging to "the fourth kingdom," and the "ten horns" of Daniel's vision, likewise belonging to "the fourth kingdom," are these same "ten kings" of John's vision—*"ten kings" out of the domain of the Empire of the Cæsars.* These "ten kings" in the last hour of "the times of the Gentiles" shall covenant to "give their power and strength unto the beast" (Rev. 17:13). They shall be overthrown when the Lion of Judah's tribe, "glorious in His apparel, traveling in the greatness of His strength," with "the day of vengeance . . . in Mine [His] heart" (Isa. 63:1-4), "shall roar out of Zion . . . the hope of His people," crushing the "multitudes, multitudes in the valley of decision" (Joel 3:14, 16), fulfilling to the letter the tremendous scene beheld by John on Patmos (Rev. 19:11-21).

The dream that is certain, and the interpretation that is sure, set forth that *"the kingdom shall be divided"* (Dan. 2:41),— the Roman Empire *"divided"* into ten kingdoms, but still the Roman Empire. The *ten* shall be *one;* just as in these United States, we have forty-eight States, each with a government and governing bodies of its own, yet all allied under one head. The forty-eight are one. These ten kingdoms must all have been found within, in order to come "out of" (Dan. 7:24) the old Roman Empire. God is going to "put in their hearts to fulfill His will" and to "have one mind, and . . . give their power and strength unto the beast" (Rev. 17:13, 17). Thus, the Roman Empire in its final form will be a federated empire of ten nations, bound together for some purpose that shall be common to them all. It is upon this federated kingdom, this ten-toed kingdom, this ten-horned kingdom, this gigantic merger with Antichrist as its superhead, its "king of kings," that "the Stone of Israel" must fall!

"The scripture cannot be broken," said the Master, even though many scoff at it. *The Roman Empire must be revived!* I believe the time is at hand!

II

"I BELIEVE IN THE RESURRECTION
OF THE EMPIRE"

IN NOVEMBER, 1925, Benito Mussolini stood before the Italian Parliament, and thundered:

"I affirm that in Fascism there are principles of life and universal character which cannot be stopped. . . . This principle is not confined to Italy, but exists for all other countries. . . . I will not menace any country, but in my capacity as chief of this government I warn the entire world. You know me as a man who does not speak, but acts!"

Again an English magazine (*Dawn*, Mar. 15, 1934) quotes him as having said in those early days of his imperial rule:

"I give to the Italian nation a hard but magnificent task, that of obtaining primacy on earth and in the skies. This primacy must be both in material things and in the spirit . . . the Fascistization of the universe!" "Powerful as in the days of the first Empire of Augustus, Rome must again become the wonder of the whole world."

Mussolini's Boasts.

A lot of people laughed, called his words "the braggadocio of a megalomaniac," "a tempest within a disordered brainpan," etc., and declared he was entitled to a diploma for being the world's foremost big-mouthed egoist. However, in those days there were others who were searching the Scriptures that they might know whereunto this thing might come. I was not quite ready to dismiss this strange son of a blacksmith and of a witch with a wave of the hand. Madman he might be; yet history is replete with evidence that a madman may be a very dangerous person, especially when in possession of implements of power.

Yes, I was interested because this new Cæsar suddenly arose *on the banks of the Tiber*. I was interested because we heard him say:

"What takes place, takes place by my precise and direct will, and according to my exact orders. I woo nobody. I reject nobody. But I trust above all in my own strength" (*Times,* London, Feb. 20, 1923).

I recalled that Daniel spoke of a king who should some day "exalt himself" and "do according to his will" (Dan. 11:36).

I was interested because we heard him say:

"A good Fascist cares nothing about elections and parliaments" (*Fellowship Forum,* Mar. 13, 1926). "A Fascist soldier has a moral law entirely unto himself. The common moral law, associated with the family, with political affairs and social relations, primitive as it is, is of no value to a Fascist soldier" (*Life of Mussolini*).

I remembered that Paul warned that the last Gentile ruler of the earth is to be that utterly "lawless one" (2 Thess. 2:8, R.V.).

I was interested when on May 26, 1927, his words were flashed around the world:

"Violence is not immoral. . . . What constitutes the State? The police. All your codes, all your doctrines, all your ordinances are as naught if at a given moment the police by sheer physical force do not make felt the inescapable weight of the law. . . . Order comes before culture; the policeman is more important than the professor. . . . Every young man, as he grows up, gets two things from me: an appointment in the ranks of the black-shirts, and what is infinitely more important, a first-class gun, with plenty of cartridges. . . . We are ready now with an army of five million men!"

We were reminded that, when the king who "shall do according to his will" shall come, the only God he will honor will be "the god of fortresses" (Dan. 11:38, R.V.).

I was interested inasmuch as we heard him say:

"My ambition is a single one. . . . Nor would it matter if I lost my life, and I should not consider it a greater sacrifice than is due. My ambition is this—to make the Italian people strong, prosperous, great, and free. . . . Rome fell and rose again. . . . Beyond the Adriatic there are the Mediterranean and other seas which can interest us. . . . The Roman Empire is a creation of the spirit, and it was the spirit which first inspired the Roman legions to fight. . . .   May God help me to carry my arduous task to a victorious end" (*Literary Digest,* Apr. 23, 1927).

The Amazing Fascist Creed.

And my interest increased tremendously when I read the closing declarations of his Fascist creed, which creed was to be committed to memory by every boy and girl in Italy:

"*I believe in the genius of Mussolini;*
"In our Holy Father Fascism and in the communion of martyrs;
"In the conversion of the Italians; and
"IN THE RESURRECTION OF THE EMPIRE."

I recalled that the ten-horned "beast" should be one who, king and kingdom, was to be "smitten unto death," but whose "death-stroke" was to be "healed" (Rev. 13:3, R.V.).

The Harlot Rides the "Beast."

I was interested when, in one of his famous speeches (May 26, 1927), this modern Roman dictator declared:

"There was but one party [in Italy] which had lingered outside the camp of Fascism. That was the Catholic party. *It has now joined the ranks of Fascism and is collaborating with Fascism and its principles all along the line."*

And shortly thereafter Cardinal Vanutelli, speaking from Rome to the world, said: "Mussolini is the man chosen by God to direct Italy to her glorious goal."   I was reminded of the fact that the Seer of Patmos beheld the "beast" meandering forth at the time of the end, with a "harlot"—ecclesiastical Rome—astride, "collaborating with Fascism" (cf. Rev. 17)! Yes, this Roman "beast" *was* interesting!

Is Mussolini Possibly the Antichrist To Be?

Weighing this man's position and power, and his words and deeds, I agreed with D. M. Panton when he wrote in the *Dawn* (Dec. 1925):

"Mussolini is either a remarkable understudy of the Seventh Emperor yet to come, or he is the man; and while probability points to his being an understudy, the fact thrills us to the soul that we cannot exclude the possibility of his being no less a person than the Seventh Emperor,"—

That is, the Antichrist himself!

I want to be understood. No man on this side of the translation of the saints will be able to point with any degree of certainty to any man and say, "There goes the Antichrist," simply because the Antichrist will not have his revelation until "that [the saints] which restraineth . . . be taken out of the way" (2 Thess. 2:6-8, R.V.). But in a day when all signs are pointing to the imminent return of our Lord, and when all Europe seems bent on setting the stage for the reign of "the beast," I believe I am speaking within bounds when I say that Benito Mussolini *is interesting*; and, to say the least, is an ominous portent.

The Roman Empire Resurrected.

Yes, the Roman Empire must be resurrected from its sleep of the centuries. So said Daniel. So said John. So agrees Mussolini. And *what do we behold?*

Only a few months ago the Roman dictator, having conquered Ethiopia against the protest of practically all the nations of the earth, annexed it to his dominions. It could not have been otherwise. God's Word stands: *"And the Ethiopians shall be at his steps"* (Dan. 11:43). He then officially announced that Italy is no longer merely a nation, but is in fact an "empire." Thus the *"Roman Empire"* is on the map— an actuality once again. True, it is not yet, in glory and power, all that it was in the days of Augustus Cæsar. Exactly that is not to be. The Roman Empire in its final form is to be a *federated* kingdom—ten nations that must become *as* one,— "ten toes"—"ten horns"—*ten states* out of the old Roman Empire, and within the new Roman Empire—*a United States of The Mediterranean.* And this is the thing that seems to be shaping itself before our very eyes. Even the unregenerate world is becoming conscious of it. The *Kansas City Star* (April 1939) said editorially:

"Benito Mussolini is reported to be basing his historic claim to dominion over Albania on the fact that this territory formed part of the Roman Empire some 2,000 years ago. *That is an interesting doctrine.* The Roman Empire at one time or another included the whole Balkan peninsula, modern Turkey, Syria, Palestine, Egypt, and most of North Africa, Spain, France, England, Switzerland, and Southern Germany. If the invasion of Albania means that the Duce has decided to reassert the ancient rights of Rome, *it looks as if he had his work cut out for him.*"

Now, out of the territory that "formed the Roman Empire some 2,000 years ago" are to come the "ten kings" that are to "have one mind, and . . . give their power and strength unto the beast" (Rev. 17:13). These are the "ten kings" that "shall make war with the Lamb" when "the Lord shall go forth, and fight against those nations," when "His feet shall stand in that day upon the mount of Olives, . . . and the Lord shall be king over all the earth" (Zech. 14:3, 4, 9. Cf. Rev. 17:14; 19:11-21).

It is of interest to note how near to that exact number—*ten* —are the kings that are even now reigning within the confines of the old Roman Empire. The boundaries are fairly well determined by the historian. If it should appear that there are *now* two or three more than ten, let it be remembered that the federation is not necessarily to come to its exact predicted number until shortly before Armageddon shall be fought. And, in these days, kingdoms are disappearing overnight. Albania, Austria, Czechoslovakia, and Poland furnish the evidence. When the hour strikes, there will be *ten.*

The "Rome-Berlin Axis."

If Adolf Hitler would consult the words of the living God instead of the stars of his pagan deities, he would know that no alliance that Germany can make with the Roman Empire will stand. Germany was never a part of the Roman Empire. Therefore, the "Rome-Berlin Axis" is foredoomed. Believe it or not, a "Rome-Paris-London Axis" is more to the point. *France and England were once a part of the Empire.*

If, years ago, I was interested in Mussolini and his dream of a resurrected Empire, I surely am interested now when I see him seemingly on the very verge of the realization of the dream. Notwithstanding the present popular idea, *the master-mind of Europe today is not in Berlin.* Neither is he in Moscow, nor Paris, nor London. The master-mind of Europe is in Rome. It was not Rome that invited a huge grizzly to park on its back doorstep. On September 19, 1939, Sir Philip Gibbs, famous war correspondent for the *New York Times,* wirelessed from London:

"The Russian Bear sprawls across the earth from east to west. In Europe this Russian crime which gave the death-blow to Poland terrifies many small nations. . . . Germany has opened her gates to the Russian Bear, who will one day bite her throat. . . . Stalin, not Hitler, will dictate terms."

It is not Rome that is divorcing the good will of the world by pouncing upon any and all small defenseless nations and gulping them down into her maw. Rome is too astute for all that. All this talk of the Roman dictator fading permanently out of the limelight, giving place to the Teuton and the Muscovite—this talk of Mussolini trailing in behind with a second fiddle—is without basis, at least, in the Scriptures. Mussolini, the Roman, is playing the shrewdest game on the international stage, today!

The Shrewd Game of the Roman Cæsar.

Let us see. This megalomaniac of fifteen years ago has resurrected his Empire, for the Roman Empire is again on the map! Not yet has his Empire gotten rid of all its graveclothes and stepped forth into its predicted glory. That is still ahead. But, nevertheless, it is here—*The Roman Empire!*

But on the one side of this Empire were two powerful enemies—Britain and France—embittered especially because of the Ethiopian steal. On the other side were two other powerful enemies—Russia and Germany—enemies because of conflicting ideologies and conflicting ambitions. Any one of these four enemies was stronger than the Roman. Now, behold that which the Roman slyly engineered!

Europe had not space enough for two Cæsars. So the Roman Cæsar invited the German Cæsar down into his domain, tickled his vanity in a glorious parade of honor, formed an "axis" with him, and sent him back to Berlin with all the swell and swagger of a Napoleon ready to "lick the world"! He promptly began trampling beneath his spurred boots the helpless states to the east. None knew better than Mussolini that this would sooner or later involve him in endless difficulties with his powerful neighbors. It did. *But the Roman, in the beginning, side-stepped the conflict!* Hitler, sensing possible desertion on the part of his Roman ally, was driven into his famous "pact" with the Russian Bear.

Soon land and sea were aquiver with the rumbling thunder of the great guns and the giant bombs of France and England on the one side, and of Germany on the other. None knew better than "the man on the white horse" in Rome that these three giants would bleed themselves white in the combat. He stood aloof, waiting to see how the fortunes of the battle would go. When France fell to her knees, bleeding at every pore, and with victory in sight for the German, the spoiler stepped in just in time to share the spoils from France with his own legions receiving scarcely a single thrust of the sword. And now, with England and Germany still locked in the throes of a struggle to the death, he is still playing around on the sidelines, keeping his boasted "eight million bayonets" bright, and his airplanes poised! He knows that *his hour will come!*

The Roman Cæsar Looking Ahead.

The shadows of the Russian Bear and the German Black Eagle fall athwart the Balkans and Turkey. They are jittery; and not without reason. The master-mind in Rome acts. Friendship and non-aggression pacts have been signed, or are in the process of swift formation. The Hungarian publicist, Sandor Petho, wrote in the Budapest newspaper, *Magyar Nemzet,* declaring that the small nations of southeastern Europe are pinning their hopes on Italy as being their defense in case of emergency. He writes:

"Italy does not end at the Alps or the Balkan mountains. She goes to the Carpathians, which now are threatened with barbarian forces. Rome is building and fortifying the bomb-proof shelter of European civilization. Rome's eyes are centered on small peoples on whose life the shadow of social revolution and Pan-Slavism lengthens."

Pardon us, Mr. Petho, but Rome's eyes are centered on more than a few *"small"* peoples." Rome's eyes are centered *on the dream*—"THE RESURRECTION OF THE EMPIRE" —*"glorious as in the days of Augustus Cæsar"*! Mussolini today, as the giants about him struggle and weaken, is burning the midnight oil, forming his "bloc." Ostensibly, it is to pre-serve small states from the insatiable jaws of Gog and his allies. As the great Bear is gorged with the warm blood of Estonia, Latvia, Lithuania, and Finland, even so the great Black Eagle is gorged with the yet warmer blood of Austria, Czechoslovakia, Poland, Norway, Denmark, Holland, Belgium, and France. And now both the Bear and the Black Eagle glance glutton-ously at Rumania. And beyond Rumania, lie Bulgaria, Yugo-slavia, Greece, Turkey, Syria, Palestine, and Egypt. It is apparent that *something must be done* or shortly the whole earth will lie within the stinking insides of these two great belly-gods! *Mankind needs a saviour!*

Now, no matter what his present opportune alliances may be, nobody knows better than the Roman dictator that *something must be done* to save *himself* from the insatiable maws of these two totalitarian gormandizers. For, when they have swallowed all Europe down to the "boot," they will not be averse to gulp-ing down the "boot" itself!

Mussolini's proposed bloc, I believe, will be the answer. I may safely predict that the bloc, when complete, will not in-clude merely the Southern Balkan states—it will finally extend westward as well. Spain and Portugal are there. Also watch for this: France and England to be forced, by arms, or other-wise, to pay the price—probably railway passage from Ethiopia to the sea, the port of Djibouti, and equality in the Suez. With that, they also, "to save civilization," to guarantee the safety of the world from enslavement by the northern colossus and his allies, will join the "bloc." "Ten kings" having "one mind" will complete the bloc. *Then,* Rome restored, the last Gentile Cæsar will reign for one short "hour." *Then* the "Stone of Israel" will fall! *Then* the Gentile colossus, beheld by Nebuchadnezzar, with all his "excellent" power and glory will pass! *Then* the Kingdom of God will come! *Then* "sorrow and sighing shall flee away"! *Then,* come, Lord Jesus, come!

III

A UNION THAT ASTOUNDED THE WORLD

HUMAN events are impelling the world forward to a destiny fixed within the eternal purposes of God, with a speed that bewilders and dazzles the mind of man. The divine plan of God is the same as it was when first declared by God through His prophets from two to four millenniums ago—unchanged and unchangeable. But the current events that are fulfilling God's purposes rush upon each other's heels so fast that they are almost stale before they can be rushed into print.

The Purpose of a New Federation of Roman States.

I have set forth that the dictator of the Roman Empire (a post *now* held by Benito Mussolini) will forsake Adolf Hitler, and ignore the solemn covenant in the "Rome-Berlin Axis" just as soon as such action will mean the furtherance of the ambitious purposes of Rome. At a psychological moment, he will step in with the "eight million bayonets," and, on the plea that it will be the only way to "save civilization" from a new series of invasions like those under Genghis Khan and Timour (Tamerlane)—invasions when "the King of the North" shall mobilize a possible seventeen millions of savage, semi-civilized Bolshevists—he will propose the re-creation of the old Roman

Empire. As we have seen, this empire will be re-created in all of its ancient power through "ten kings," reigning within the boundaries of that ancient empire, having "one mind" and giving "their power and strength unto the beast" (Rev. 17:13).

Now, no "ten kings" will ever be persuaded to surrender their sovereignty to any dictator, yielding to him their utmost power and strength, unless they have some compelling reason. "Gog" and his allies (Ezek. 38 and 39) will furnish that very good and compelling reason. It is said that Russia can mobilize seventeen million men within three months. The *Berlin Vorstoss,* before the recent Russo-German pact became a fact, declared: "In the teeming brain of Stalin are shaped dreams no less ambitious than were the longings for world sway of an Alexander the Great or a Napoleon." And the truth of those words is more evident today than ever before.

The *Los Angeles Times* (Nov. 18, 1939) printed a dispatch from Rome under the headline: "Mussolini Orders New Army Increases as Soviet Is Defied." We read:

"Premier Mussolini today ordered a further increase in the strength of the standing army, which the Fascist press said is being made as formidable as possible *so that Italy will be able to 'SAY THE LAST WORD' when the time comes to make peace in Europe.*"

Exactly so! And the world certainly ought to know by this time what that "last word" will be! It has been declared often enough for nearly a score of years:

"My ambition is a single one. . . . Nor would it matter if I lost my life, and I should not consider it a greater sacrifice than is due. . . . Powerful as in the days of the first Empire of Augustus, Rome must again become the wonder of the whole world."

"Peace in Europe" must come and be maintained through the mighty power of a restored Roman Empire. I venture to say that nothing less than *that* will be "the last word" of "the man on the white horse" in Rome. The centralization of the armed might of all the Mediterranean states into the hands of one man will be accepted as the only way out of the international distress.

But those who stand within the counsels of the God Who sees the end from the beginning are well aware that "when they shall say, Peace and safety; then sudden destruction cometh upon them" (I Thess. 5:3).

Not Enough Room for Two Cæsars.

This same dispatch out of Rome carried a warning to Soviet Russia. It was printed in the Fascist party newspaper, *Regima Fascista,* of Cremona. It said:

"Finland is menaced by Russia, who wants to profit from the situation in the Baltic and return to the status of imperial times. In this conflict we naturally sympathize with the small, heroic Finnish nation. . . . Finland has contented herself with her legitimate historic territory."

It might be well to inquire of Ethiopia what she thinks of any Italian sympathy "for a small, heroic nation." It is quite evident that the trouble with Benito Mussolini is that he cannot see how there can be sufficient room in Europe for two Cæsars both enjoying "the status of imperial times"!

On November 17, 1939, bitter attacks were broadcast from Rome, and were heard over Europe, solemnly warning the Russian Bear to keep his nose out of the Balkan pie, and away from the waters of the Danube. All this fits perfectly into the divine program, setting the stage as the prophets declared it would be set for the Gentile sunset. I repeat: *as certainly as the Russo-German pact had to come into existence, even so the "Rome-Berlin Axis" has to break;* but not until that "Axis" has accomplished its purpose under God.

The "Pact" That Astounded the World.

On August 23, 1939, an event took place that surprised and stunned the world as no other event in modern times has done. That event was the signing of the non-aggression pact between Nazi Germany and Communist Russia. It was signed right at the moment when the official representatives of England and

France were sitting at the door of Stalin's office, ready and expecting to do the signing themselves.

G. E. R. Gedye, correspondent for the *New York Times*, wired from Moscow on September 30, 1939:

"Never in the course of history were so many millions metaphorically knocked off their feet by a single political development, as when on the morning of August 22 people read in their newspapers that Herr von Ribbentrop, German Foreign Minister, was flying to Moscow to sign a non-aggression pact between the two opposing worlds of Nazism and Communism. It was not only the seemingly irreconcilable ideological conflict which upset the calculations of friends and foes of each country, but the fact that Russia had constantly taken the lead in resistance to Germany's aggression and had vainly demanded international action against her."

The *New York Times* itself said editorially on October 1, 1939:

"The alliance between Germany and Russia is a development that would have been thought incredible as late as two or three months ago, not only by the majority of peoples in other countries, but by the overwhelming majority of Germans and Russians themselves. The first country represented Fascism, the second Communism, each in its most extreme form. For years each of these two systems had been represented as the exact antithesis and only formidable enemy of the other in what each had declared to be a life-and-death struggle. . . . Both Stalin and Hitler certainly completely distrust each other, and for the very strongest of reasons. . . . If army circles, as our Berlin correspondent informs us, 'frankly declare' that Germany must now 'prepare for the inevitable dispute with Soviet Russia that must come some day,' we may be sure that the opinion is shared by other elements in the population."

On the same day that the Russo-German pact was signed, Leon Blum, very recently Premier of France, said to the world:

"It is difficult to dissimulate my stupefaction! . . . incredible and virtually stupefying! One is doubly astonished when one remembers that horror and hate of Communism are the feelings by which Hitler has endeavored to justify all his recent enterprises."

From London came an Associated Press dispatch, declaring that the Russo-German pact represents "one of the most astounding and shocking reversals of policy in history," and that it left all the other nations of Europe "stunned."

On August 24, 1939, the well-known columnist, Paul Mallon, wrote from Washington:

"When a friend phoned a Russian expert of this Government the news that the Communists had made some kind of a marriage settlement with the Nazis, he refused to believe it. Next day, after reading official announcements of the nuptials from Berlin and Moscow, he still refused to believe it, but with a small cough-laugh that indicated his doubt might continue even after the text had been made public, and the child born, if any. This little minor incident is all revealing of the extent of the shock felt on high here."

All the world knows that Adolf Hitler rode into dictatorial power on a platform demanding the suppression of Communism, which the German people believed absolutely necessary if civilization was not to be dissolved! As for the Communistic hordes of Russia, Mussolini they have not loved, but Hitler they have hated! The very suggestion that an alliance would some day be formed whereby the German Black Eagle and the Russian Bear would roost peacefully together on the same limb, was a suggestion that could come only from a mind of dense ignorance or bereft of all reason! It seemed beyond all comprehension that any one or two men could rise to power in this advanced age, who would cast to the winds their principal theses and justifications for the leadership of mighty nations, and unite their forces in violation of every political tenet for which they ever stood.

God Moves Kings at Will.

We have taken the space to quote extensively here, to show how our God, when the time comes for Him to move onward in the course He has indicated by His prophets, laughs at all that men call "impossible," and moves the mightiest of kings and dictators at will. No ideology, no doctrine, no alliance that man knows, hinders in the least the Lord God of Israel from fulfilling His eternal purpose in Christ. "The Most High God ruleth in the kingdom of men, and . . . setteth up over it whomsoever He will" (Dan. 5:21). And sometimes, in the mystery of His ways, as today, He chooses to set up "over it the basest of men" (Dan. 4:17).

Then:

"Why do the nations rage, and the peoples meditate a vain thing? The kings of the earth set themselves, and the rulers take counsel together, against Jehovah, and against His anointed, saying, Let us break their bonds asunder, and cast away their cords from us. He that sitteth in the heavens will laugh: the Lord will have them in derision. . . . Now therefore be ye wise, O ye kings: be instructed, ye judges of the earth" (Psalm 2:1-4, 10, R.V.).

The unregenerate of this world's intelligentsia, political experts who consider their wisdom to exceed that of other human beings, have long assured us that Germany and Russia could never march together to battle. But those who believe that the wisdom of God is greater than all the wisdom of men have been telling us for fifty years past that when the final hour of this age strikes, Germany (Gomer) will march with Russia (Gog) against the Jew in Palestine. Therefore, some of us were not "stunned" in the least when we saw the talon of the German Black Eagle, gory with the flesh and blood of Israel, reach forth to clasp the blood-begrimed paw of the Russian Bear. Rather, we rejoiced in that we see the day swiftly approaching when Satan's monstrous rule over the nations shall come to its predestined end. Time ever vindicates the truth of God.

Back in 1934, at the request of some friends, I printed a sermon I had preached on the subject, "God and Gog." On page 19 of that little booklet is the following:

"Many German editors insist that Germany can never march with the Bolsheviki. But stranger things than that have happened. Strange forces are at work these days in a world more afflicted with revolution and devolution than with evolution.

When the hour strikes, Germany will tramp, Hitler and his Fascist brown shirts notwithstanding, with . . . *Gog!*"

More than that, when the hour strikes, as I have always said, the German Black Eagle will not fly as a screaming air pilot ahead of the old Russian Bear. Rather, that Eagle, with wings duly clipped, will be a tagtail, waddling along behind the Bear. I was not a prophet in 1934, even as I am not a prophet now. I simply believe that God's Word cannot fail, even to its last jot and tittle. I shall reserve for the next chapter the story of the outcome of the Russo-German pact. In the meantime, I set forth once again that there is only one sure reason why the Russian Bear forsook all companionship with the British Lion, and joined himself in companionship to a bird as unclean as himself: *"Now all this is come to pass, that it might be fulfilled which was spoken by the Lord through the prophet"* (Matt. 1:22, R.V.).

And more "incredible and stupefying," more "astounding and shocking" events are still ahead of us, before "all that the prophets have spoken" shall have come to pass. But through them all, God will remain upon His throne, and His true saints have nothing to worry about. We can safely leave the future to Him Who ever careth for His own!

IV

EZEKIEL'S GREAT PROPHECY CONCERNING "GOG" AND "GOMER"

NO MODERN nation is set forth so vividly in the prophetic Word as is Russia. Probably the reason is that the Eternal, looking down across the sands of time, beheld Russia, as no other nation, raising her mighty fists and hissing her defiance. It is recalled that Stalin, the Neronic dictator of Russia, signed the official decree back in 1932 ordering the Almighty to pack His few remaining belongings and get out of the Soviet empire!   That decree, according to the London *Morning Post,* read:

"On May 1, 1937, there must not remain on the territory of the U.S.S.R. a single house of prayer to God, and the very conception 'God' will be banished from the boundaries of the Soviet Union, as a survival of the Middle Ages which has served as an instrument for the oppression of the working masses."

The date is past!   We have not as yet heard that the Almighty took His exit!

Ezekiel Sets His Face Toward Gog.

Beholding this gory monster, whose deeds of cruelty, lust, and blood were not surpassed by even Ivan the Terrible, or Nero, or any other human beast known to history, need we wonder that the God of Israel, foreseeing him, gave the order to Ezekiel:

"Son of man, set thy face toward Gog, of the land of Magog, the prince of Rosh, Meshech, and Tubal, and prophesy against him, and say, Thus saith the Lord Jehovah: Behold, I am against thee, O Gog, prince of Rosh, Meshech, and Tubal" (Ezek. 38:1-3, R. V.)

So many great scholars have shown conclusively that Russia and her latter day allies are the "Gog" of Ezekiel that it seems unnecessary to take space here with further discussion of the subject.   Scofield, referring to Ezekiel's prophecy, rightly says: "That the primary reference is to the northern (European) powers, headed up by Russia, *all agree.* . . . The reference to Meshech and Tubal (Moscow and Tobolsk) is a clear mark of identification."

The Allies of Gog.

A matter more necessary here is to identify these allies of Gog as they are named on the sacred page:

"Persia, Cush, and Put with them. . . . Gomer, and all his hordes; the house of Togarmah in the uttermost parts of the north, and all his hordes" (Ezek. 38:5,6, R.V.).

Persia needs no identification. Persia today is allied with Russia. She has entered into an agreement with the northern Goliath that, should Britain attack him, Persia will provide him with a highway to India. Cush and Put (not the Ethiopia and Libya countries of Africa, as many reading the Authorized Version infer) are not clearly identified. But they were evidently provinces within or near Persia. The *International Standard Bible Encyclopedia* says that Cush is "the name of the country around which the Gihon flowed (Gen. 2:13), rendered 'Ethiopia' in the Authorized Version."

As for Togarmah, Jewish writers (probably correctly) call the Turks "Togarmah." But Turkey, as we know it, is not in view here. Note carefully that it is "Togarmah *in the uttermost parts of the north*." I accept the view of many writers that the Togarmah of Ezekiel is our present Turkestan, which is one of the Soviet Republics today.

Who Is "Gomer"?

As for Gomer, in Genesis 10:3 we are told that Gomer had three sons, Riphath, Togarmah, Ashkenaz. Gomer and his tribe sojourned from Asia Minor to the north coast of the Black Sea. The place where they settled was first called Gomeria, then Cimmeria, and later Crimea, which is its name today. Ashkenaz moved up the Danube and peopled what is known today as Germany. Webster says that Gomer was "a northern people from the Armenian highlands, identified with the *Gimirrai* of the cuneiform inscriptions." The Jews today call their brethren from Germany "Askenazim," after Ashkenaz, son of Gomer. The Jewish Talmud supports this view. Gomer is there stated to be the Germani, that is, Germany.

If we are correct in the location of these peoples, then it is intensely interesting to know that after twenty-five centuries these peoples are all allied with Russia today. Kaleidoscopic they may have been through the centuries; yet today they settle into the pattern foretold by the prophet so long ago.

We now see how it is that, while the recent pact formed between Germany and Russia "stunned" England, and "stupefied" France, and "shocked" the whole world, nevertheless, it caused no surprise whatever to those who know the prophets. I have just unearthed the *Christian Herald* of November 7, 1917—twenty-two years ago. The late Dr. James M. Gray, then Dean of the Moody Bible Institute of Chicago, wrote on the subject, *"What the Bible Teaches about Russia."* At that time Russia had just tossed aside the Czarist yoke. On the basis of Ezekiel's prophecy, Dr. Gray said:

"He [the writer] rejoices with Russia in her new-found freedom. . . . But he is obliged to add, as a faithful interpreter of the Word of God, that he would not be surprised if democracy in Russia were short-lived. . . . The Bible seems to fore-shadow this. And, indeed, that Russia should at length be found in alliance with Germany, or Germany with her, is not one of the improbabilities, judging from the same source. . . . Of course, dogmatic assertions are out of place, but if our interpretation of Ezekiel be correct, then the present alliance of Russia with the western nations is not likely to be permanent, for they are of the original Roman Empire, to which she never belonged. And for this reason it is more likely that one of these days the relationship of Russia and Germany shall become close; for Germany, like Russia, was never of the Roman Empire, except as to that part of her territory west of the Rhine."

Apparently, the preacher who sticks to the Word of God, no matter though its prophecies may at the time seem to man impossible of fulfilment, has no need to make apologies as the revealing years come along. God, looking down across the sands of time and beholding this northern leviathan that boasts of 17,000,000 muskets today, cried: "I am against thee, O Gog"! Today Gog raises his fist toward the heavens and cries: "And I am against thee, O God!" And the fight is on—a fight that will end only when God shall "give unto Gog a place for burial in Israel . . . [in] the valley of Hamon-gog" (Ezek. 39:11, 15). Yes, this present-day battle against God by the Russian bolshevistic nullifidians is but a part of the prophetic program, running as true to the "sure word of prophecy" as the needle runs true to the pole.

"Clothed in Full Armor."

"O Gog, prince of Rosh, . . . I will turn thee about, and put hooks into thy jaws, and will bring thee forth, and all thine army, horses and horsemen, all of them clothed in full armor, a great company with buckler and shield, all of them handling swords" (Ezek. 38:3, 4, R.V.).

The *Sunday School Times,* on December 16, 1939, editorially called attention to a very interesting fact in connection with Ezekiel's statement that the Russian hordes will come forth *"clothed in full armor."* In this day of advanced military science and equipment, cumbersome armor such as was worn in Biblical times has been supposed to belong to the relics of the past. Therefore, it was feared that one prophet erred in his statement. But the *Science News Letter* (Oct. 7, 1939) published an article under the head of "Military Science," with the title, *"Armor May Become Fashion Even Among Civil Population."* (We need only to recall recent pictures of civilians to confirm this—pictures showing vast civilian populations in Europe in protective dress, the most hideous of which is the gas mask.) We quote from the article:

"Wearing of armor like that of knights of old, only proof against modern bullets and shell fragments, is likely to come into fashion again, even among the civil population, predicts Stephen V. Grancsay, curator of arms and armor in the Metropolitan Museum of Art.

"Armored men have already been reported as having been seen repairing the barbed wire in front of German entrenchments on the western front.

"'Armor wearing is not ideal,' Mr. Grancsay stated to *Science Service*. 'However, a soldier necessarily has to bear great discomforts. I am sure that with the light alloys developed today armor will be used extensively, even by the civilians as a protection against flying debris. Armor would be effective against the shells falling from anti-aircraft guns. . . .

" 'Every soldier in all armies these days wears a helmet, and if a helmet is good protection,' Mr. Grancsay reasons, 'why should not other body armor be equally good protection?'

"Mr. Grancsay has the backing of no less an authority than General Pershing, whom he quotes: 'Effort should be continued towards the development of a satisfactory form of personal armor.'

"Two and a half years ago, on April 7, 1937, Mr. Grancsay predicted the return of body armor, in a *Science Service* radio broadcast."

After all, "the sure word of prophecy" will be vindicated by the fulfilment of its minutest details to the last "jot and tittle" (Matt. 5:18).

Russia's "Horses and Horsemen."

And again the prophecy runs true. Newspaper correspondents with the Russian army that overran eastern Poland wrote descriptions of that army. The modern army, even as the German army that overran western Poland, is "motorized." And much of the Russian army is modern. But, in addition to its motorized battalions, the Russian army is accompanied by great masses of cavalry. The latter-day enemies of Israel that shall sweep out of the north parts are ever accompanied with "horses and horsemen": "And thou shalt come from thy place out of the uttermost parts of the north . . . riding upon horses" (Ezek. 38:15, R.V.). "And the king of the north shall come against him like a whirlwind, with chariots, and with horsemen" (Dan. 11:40). As a matter of fact, the terrain down over which Gog and his hordes must march, out of Russia, down past the cedars of Lebanon into the land of Israel, to "take a spoil," will find the horse superior to the tank. Correspondents have told us that the Russian army in eastern Poland presented rather a "strange appearance." The Russians looked more like an Asiatic horde than a modern European army. And this exactly fits into the prophetic picture drawn by Ezekiel.

While our Western Powers bemoan the fact that Poland should have been caught in a pincers movement between these two northern titans and crushed to death, it must not be forgotten that these titans, and all other titanic powers, are utterly in the hands of the Lord God of Israel. Hear God speak to Gog: *"I will turn thee about, and put hooks into thy jaws, and I will bring thee forth"* (Ezek. 38:4, R.V.). Thank God for the assurance that, as those great foamy-jawed beasts of the north countries go prowling forth from their dens, the hooks of our God are in their jaws! We have no need of fear!

The Mighty Hand Behind the Scenes.

Once upon a time, in the long ago, a prophet of God said of the mightiest ruler of that day: *"Cyrus, he is My shepherd, and shall perform all My pleasure: even saying to Jerusalem, Thou shalt be built; and to the temple, Thy foundation shall be laid"* (Isa. 44:28). And thus a pagan world-ruler, who was ever an enemy of the Jew, was compelled to rebuild the city of the Jew, and to lay the foundation of the temple of the Jew!

To another prophet God spoke of the Babylonian enemy of Israel thus: "Nebuchadnezzar the king of Babylon, *My servant"!* (Jer. 25:9; 27:6). And once upon a time this Nebuchadnezzar, "head of gold," mightiest monarch of them all, swaggered about, boasting of this "great Babylon, that I have built" (Dan. 4:30)! The Mighty One of Israel looked down from His throne in the skies and said to that monarch: "Will you please go out into the fields, fall down upon your all-fours, and eat greens for seven years until you know that there is a God in the heavens Who 'ruleth in the kingdom of men, and giveth it to whomsoever He will, and setteth up over it the basest of men'?" (Dan. 4:17). And that old self-deified Babylonian trotted off into the fields like an obedient little boy, fell upon his all-fours, and chewed greens and grew hair like eagles' feathers until he was ready to return to his palace and proclaim to the world:

"Nebuchadnezzar the king, unto all people, nations, and languages, that dwell in all the earth; Peace be multiplied unto you. . . . Now I Nebuchadnezzar praise and extol and honour the King of heaven, all Whose works are truth, and His ways judgment: and those that walk in pride He is able to abase" (Dan. 4:1, 37).

"Shall Not the Judge . . . Do Right?"

Then, ye saints of God, take courage! While one cannot but pity Poland for that which has befallen her, let it not be forgotten that Poland sinned grievously in recent years in her bitter persecution of Israel, the chosen of God. Judgment for her was certain, as it will be for all others that lay violent hands upon God's "anointed" (I Chron. 16:22). Verily, Nebuchadnezzar was right: "Whose works are truth, and His ways *judgment*"! God used Nebuchadnezzar to judge a disobedient people, and then punished the wicked instrument used in that judgment.

Beyond question the days of judgment are falling upon the nations that have counted Christ out of their counsels. Therefore, God permits the "basest of men" to rule over them. But, judging the future from the past, some of Europe's autocrats, now being used of God in His judgments, shall be put on a diet of greens! It would at least be somewhat satisfying to have the assurance that in that day that is coming soon, a certain triumvirate in Europe may be compelled to issue a proclamation before they bow their necks for the final stroke of their doom:

"WE, STALIN, HITLER, AND MUSSOLINI, UNTO ALL PEOPLE, NATIONS, AND LANGUAGES, THAT DWELL IN ALL THE EARTH; PEACE BE MULTIPLIED UNTO YOU. NOW WE PRAISE AND EXTOL AND HONOUR THE LORD GOD OF ABRAHAM, ISAAC, AND JACOB, EVEN THE LORD GOD OF THE JEW, AND HAVE LEARNED THAT THOSE THAT WALK IN PRIDE HE IS ABLE TO ABASE"!

V

THE RUSSIAN COLOSSUS CROSSES THE RUBICON

IN THE Jewish magazine *Opinion,* (Sept., 1939) of which Rabbi Stephen S. Wise is editor, there appeared an article by James Waterman Wise, under the caption—"Russia Betrays Mankind." This Jewish author said:

"Four years ago, in a series of articles published in *Opinion,* I stated that the Soviet Union was a powerful force for social progress and for world peace. Since then, although never a member of the Communist Party or in any way affiliated to it, I have urged American co-operation with, and support of Russia's anti-Fascist pro-democratic policy. The recently signed German-Soviet Pact and the concurrent trade treaties constitute complete reversal of that policy and abandonment of the principles on which it is based . . .

"By this pact, the Soviet Union has betrayed mankind. . . .

"In view of these facts, it behooves those of us who mistakenly believed that the present Soviet government would stand shoulder to shoulder with the democracies against Nazi-Fascism to admit our error and revise our course. . . .

"By making this pact, the Soviet Union strikes hands with a government on whose head is the innocent blood of thousands of Jews and the broken lives of hundreds of thousands more. . . .

"Disillusionment, however, need not lead to demoralization. Rather, it should compel us to re-think our problem and re-form our ranks."

More Disillusionment for Israel Ahead.

What a pity that any intelligent Jew should ever have looked to the blood-soaked colossus of the north as a hope "for social progress and for world peace," or, for friendship for his race. Every Jew has access to the words of his ancient prophets. If they must refuse to read and believe the messages of Christ and His apostles, then what a pity that they do not read and believe the messages of Moses and the prophets.

The sad "error" Mr. Wise admittedly made four years ago in his appraisal of Russia should cause him and his brethren in Israel to exercise greater caution, and go to their prophets for wisdom. But, closing their eyes to the sure words of their prophets, a sadder "error" is ahead of them.

The Lord Jesus said to the Jews in His day: "I am come in My Father's name, and ye receive Me not: if another shall come in his own name, him [the Antichrist] ye will receive" (John 5:43, R.V.). In that day, which will witness the pouring out of the "blood of thousands of Jews and the broken lives of hundreds of thousands more"—in that "time of Jacob's trouble" (Jer. 30:7)—once again there will come "disillusionment," but, at what a price!

Verily, Russia, the mighty "Gog" of Ezekiel, is no friend to Israel! Rather, she has been the most implacable foe of Judah in recent times. What are we to think of the "Christian" anti-Semites who have been trying to make the world believe that "the Jews took over Russia" in keeping with a certain program laid down in the "Protocols," and have been controlling that notorious government as their tool in disrupting all Gentile governments and communizing the world? Know they not that the god of the Russian Communist, Vladimir Lenin, died like a madman, crying out his hatred: "Kill the Jews! Kill the Jews!" And, again, consider all this talk of a Jew-controlled Russia, in the light of the fact that its Gentile tyrant, Josef Stalin, a born anti-Semite, recently forced the resignation of Maxim Litvinov as foreign commissar—*the last Jew to hold any high office in Soviet Russia.*

It is true that the new Soviet constitution provides freedom for the racial and religious groups in Russia. Nevertheless, anti-Semitism is as widespread in that unhappy land as it was in the days of Czar Nicholas II. The OGPU, or Secret Police, in their hunt for gold or foreign currency, have seized the Jews at will, and have hurled them into torture chambers until they revealed the hiding places of their wealth. George Adams, in a copyrighted article in the *Daily Mirror,* informs us that, in 1915, Litvinov, while lunching with him in Geneva, said of a certain American Jewish newspaperman: "Stalin doesn't like him! In fact, *he doesn't like any of our people!*"

Let it be remembered that Russia, in her ambitious ride to world power, stands revealed in the Word of God as the foremost of all the latter-day enemies of Israel except for the Antichrist himself, whose enmity will not appear until after the Jews shall refuse to worship his image (Rev. 13:11-18).

The Man of Steel.

It may be of interest here to know something of the personal characteristics of this blood-drunken beast whose awful shadow is terrorizing the whole world in this present hour. G. Bessyedovsky, former Soviet Ambassador to Paris, is a Russian who ought to know whereof he speaks. He says of Stalin:

"Three years ago, he decided to get rid of his old wife and to take a young one. . . .

"What became of his old wife, I do not know. . . . Few people saw his old wife, and few see his new one. Stalin keeps her at Gorki in seclusion, as in an Oriental harem. He is a despot not only in politics, but also in friendship and in love. He is pitiless in both these feelings. Here, too, he has the characteristics of an Asiatic satrap who tolerates no obstacles in his path. When his old friend Kamo, with whom he organized armed raids on banks in the days of Czarism, was recently run over by an automobile in Tiflis, Stalin, in wrath, sent a telegram to the Tiflis OGPU. 'Shoot the driver at once.' Although the driver was not at fault, and although he was also a Communist, he was shot without trial. When Pyatakov, a noted Communist, fell seriously ill from the excess of drinking, Stalin, beside himself with anger, called the physicians and ordered them: 'Cure him in two weeks!' *And Pyatakov was cured!*"

And upon such a demonized being, millions of humans— and it is regrettable that many of them were Jews—pinned their hope for a better world! Mr. Bessyedovsky, ten years ago, told us that Stalin was working under the delusion that it is his life's work to maintain the unity of the Communist party until the day shall come when, despite all setbacks, world revolution will set the earth on fire. And, probably, in the opinion of the world's foremost firebug, that hour is near! It is estimated that he has an army which, mobilized to its full strength, will put 25,000,000 men and women on his battle front—the largest military force in the world.

Gog's Final Attack on Israel.

One thing sure, when the hour does come, Israel will be the prime object of his satanic hate. It will not be against the shores of the Briton that he will hurl his massed millions, but against the mountains of Israel in "the navel of the earth." The immutable Word of God settles that!

> "O Gog, prince of Rosh, Meshech [Moscow], and Tubal [Tobolsk]. . . . Thus saith the Lord, Jehovah: It shall come to pass in that day, that things shall come into thy mind . . . and thou shalt say, I will go up to the land of unwalled villages . . . to take the spoil and to take the prey; to turn thy hand against the waste places that are now inhabited, and against the people that are gathered out of the nations, that have gotten cattle and goods, that dwell in the middle [R.V. margin, Heb., *navel*] of the earth. . . . Thou shalt come from thy place out of the uttermost parts of the north, thou, and many peoples with thee, all of them riding upon horses, a great company and a mighty army; and thou shalt come up against My people Israel, as a cloud to cover the land: it shall come to pass in the latter days" (Ezek. 38:3, 10-16, R.V.).

Gog Also Seeks World Dominion.

As we have set forth from time to time, it is not Germany, but Russia, that is to be the Goliath of the end time, that will compel other nations to form a colossal federation to preserve them from its tyrannous power. Germany will march as an ally of the northern colossus, probably because she will find herself in a position where she is unable to do anything else. Some day the German people will come to know what a stupendous error Adolf Hitler made when he entered into the recent non-aggression pact with the wily northern Bear, and destroyed Poland, the buffer state.

In the light of the revelation of the God Who knows the end from the beginning, how significant are the events of the hour! Russia, like Germany, and like Italy, is on the march to what she, at least, believes will be world empire.

Following in the wake of Peter the Great, Stalin is sweeping victoriously over the eastern Baltic, which Germany has long regarded as her own private lake. In eastern Europe, without wasting any of his powder, Stalin has raised his flag over former White Russia and the Polish Ukraine, with a larger area and population than our own New England States. More recently still, he has incorporated Estonia, Latvia, and Lithuania into the Soviet Empire. He has proceeded to force a humiliating treaty, giving him air and naval bases in Finland. The peoples of Norway and Sweden also are terrorized at the specter. Well they may be, for the "king of the north" (Dan. 11:40) will be just that—*the king of the north.*

In the Far East, the Muscovite seems to have come to an understanding with Japan. Certainly, the Russian Bear has lost his fear of events in that part of his vast den. Probably Russia's "rights" in western China, already bolshevized, are to be duly recognized by Japan.

With the situation satisfactory at each end of her vast domain, Russia is in a position to strike for the coveted warm waters of southern seas. *And it is this southward march she would avoid if she knew the prophets of God which she thoroughly despises.*

When Gog Crosses the Rubicon.

All the world expects that, since Stalin has blocked the pathway of the German army into the Balkans, especially Rumania, he will not hesitate to continue to strike for the completion of his dream of world empire in that direction. Bessarabia already has fallen a victim to the ravenous appetite of the great Bear. Doubtless, Rumania will be his next morsel. But here is where the real troubles of the Bear will begin. Here he will cross the Rubicon. The Roman Cæsar will unsheath his sword.

Not so long ago the streets of Rome and Milan teemed with

paraders, mostly students, who flew Italian and Finnish flags, shouting: *"Long live Finland!   Down with Russia, Stalin, and Bolshevism!"*   This might not mean much at certain times; but in this hour it may mean much indeed.   It means that "the king of the north" is stirring the wrath of the mighty willful king whose destiny is fixed by the Lord of heaven and earth: "He shall prosper till the indignation [of God] be accomplished" (Dan. 11:36).

This much is certain: something, sooner or later, must furnish the motive power to drive together "ten kings" and cause them to do an unprecedented thing, that is, to *"have one mind, and . . . give their power and strength unto the beast"* (Rev. 17:13).

Rome's Hour at Hand.

For some months now, Mussolini the Loquacious, has been sitting tight-lipped, nodding acquiescence and shrugging his shoulders as his "friend Hitler" booted things around according to his own good pleasure in Central Europe.   But let no one believe that the Roman's heart enters into the militaristic parades of the German cock of the walk.

However, the sagacious Mussolini knew that the opportunity would come, and come it has.   Will he grasp it?   He hasn't been famous for letting opportunities pass by.   Mussolini, the Roman, finds himself sitting in a pretty fine spot from which to draw some desirable concessions from England and France.   The shadow of the great northern Cyclops falls over the earth.   The world is trembling in a miasma of fear. That fear is so great that, with plenty of trouble already on their hands, France, England, America, and all other nations have held back aghast from doing their moral duty, and breaking off all relations with the northern brute, who, to satisfy his craven, lustful appetite, without the slightest provocation, blew men, women, and little children to bits in Helsinki; or sent them—nearly 300,000 of them—out into the Arctic forest fastnesses of Finland to perish in the sub-zero cold, while the skies behind them were reddened with the glow of the flames that devoured their once happy homes.

A predatory brute that has once tasted warm blood, and has gotten away with it unpunished, is the most dangerous of all brutes. Will "ten kings," all of whose hearts are aquiver with fear, finally be driven, even against their wills, to form the alliance that was foretold by the prophets of God in all the ages past? Is the hour at hand?

"O my Lord, what shall be the end of these things?" (Dan. 12:8).

We shall see!

VI

WHEN RUSSIA MARCHES TO HER DOOM

LET us pause to review what we have seen in Ezekiel's vision, as his God enabled him to peer ahead into the future, twenty-five centuries in advance of his day. Who among us would not be interested in envisioning the events of the year 4500 A.D.? What an amazing scene we would behold! Let us first understand the events of 1940 A.D., as God gives us wisdom from His immutable Word. Once again we have before us the prophecy of Ezekiel, Chapter 38, Revised Version.

Verse 2. *"Son of man, set thy face toward Gog, of the land of Magog, the prince of Rosh, Meshech, and Tubal, and prophesy against him."*

All agree that the Russian Empire is the subject of this prophecy.

Verse 3. *"Thus saith the Lord Jehovah: Behold, I am against thee, O Gog, prince of Rosh, Meshech, and Tubal."*

Soviet Russia is the only sovereign State known to history that ever *officially* declared war upon all that is called God. The living God accepted the challenge. That war against God, long delayed, is now on. How long will it last? No one can tell. But, in the end, God will probably win!

Verse 4. *"I will turn thee about, and put hooks into thy jaws, and I will bring thee forth."*

It is comforting to know that the raging grizzly of the North has a hook in his jaws, and that Omnipotence has His hand on the chain. In which case we are not worrying.

"The Most High Ruleth."

Once upon a time a deified bull had his stall in Babylon. God ringed that old bull, placarded his sides: "Nebuchadnezzar . . . *My servant"* (Jer. 25:9); and led him to the gates of apostate Jerusalem. Then He opened the gates and turned the old bellower loose. When the old bull stopped to breathe, he rested upon a heap of ruins. *But* when the God of Israel wanted Jerusalem built again, again He ringed a mighty bull —a Persian bull—led him to the gates of the ruined city, presented him with a yoke for a collar, and told him that that which the Gentile had destroyed the Gentile must rebuild. *And the Gentile did!* Even so it had been decreed more than two hundred years before by the God

"That saith of Cyrus, He is My shepherd, and shall perform all My pleasure, even saying of Jerusalem, She shall be built; and of the temple, Thy foundation shall be laid" (Isa. 44:28).

Verily, "Man proposes! God disposes!"

Verse 4. *"All thine army, horses and horsemen."*
And "Gog" has far more horse flesh at his command than any other nation in the world! Thus to the last jot and tittle must the Scripture be fulfilled.

Verses 5, 6. *"Persia, Cush* [probably Khuzistan, a southern province of Persia], *and Put* [probably Upper Cilicia] . . . *Gomer* [Germany, and possibly Rumania] . . . *the house of Togarmah in the uttermost parts of the north . . . with thee."*

Every one of these is an ally of "Gog" today! Is it any wonder that understanding saints are looking up, believing that "the kingdom of God is nigh"? (Luke 21:31).

Verses 11, 12. *"And thou shalt say, I will go up to the
land of unwalled villages* [Palestine] *. . . to take the
spoil and to take the prey; to turn thy hand against the
waste places that are now inhabited, and against the people that are gathered out of the nations, that have gotten
cattle and goods, that dwell in the middle of the earth."*

"Pillage"—A World-Wide Epidemic.

Thus anti-Semitism and spoliation—the two rotting diseases
with which all Gentile nations have been more or less infected
throughout the centuries—will prove utterly fatal to the
Northern Colossus. The infection of anti-Semitism and spoliation is even now an epidemic, spreading over the whole world.
It seems to have gotten beyond the best of the physicians.
They are in despair! "Is there no balm in Gilead; is there
no physician there?" (Jer. 8:22).

The old German, General Blücher, who helped the English
defeat Napoleon at Waterloo, was once invited by Lord Wellington to visit London. In showing him the city, Wellington
took him up into the dome of St. Paul's. "Well, what do you
think of it?" asked the famous duke. The blood of ten gen-
erations stirred in the veins of the old warrior, and he replied:
"What a city for pillage!"

"Pillage!" That is ever foremost in the minds of the unregenerate nations of the earth. "Pillage!" It was in the veins
of most of the nations in the World War. Mussolini, World
War veteran, caught the infection. He marched his battalions
into Ethiopia, and later into Albania, for *"pillage."* Then
Japan marched her legions into China, *for "pillage."* Germany marched into Austria, then into Czechoslovakia, then
into Poland, in quick succession, *for "pillage."* The Russian
Bear leaped from his mystic den, crushed between his sanguinary jaws Poland, Latvia, Estonia, Lithuania, and Finland
—gorging his old stomach *with "pillage"!* After Finland will
come any other little nation that the big, burly bully wants to
"pillage."

The Roman Cæsar Marches Forth, "Conquering and to Conquer."

But the end is not yet. Another despoiler must go forth, even as it is written:

> *"The king* [who] *shall do according to his will . . . shall prosper* [in spoliation] *. . . He shall enter also into the glorious land, and many countries shall be overthrown; . . . He shall stretch forth his hand also upon the countries; and the land of Egypt shall not escape. But he shall have power over the treasures of gold and of silver, and over all the precious things of Egypt"* (Dan. 11:36, 41-43).

Verily, a pillager of pillagers will be this last of the Roman Cæsars—the Antichrist! *Great Britain ought to be interested in Daniel's prophecy*—ought to be interested in the coming spoliation of Egypt. Her great fleets cannot prevent it. The march of the conqueror is overland, to the East, and then, rimming the Mediterranean, southward, on through "the glorious land" into Egypt, thus backtracking General Allenby of World War fame.

Troublesome Tidings for the Roman.

And now a very interesting thing is to take place. While this willful king from Rome shall be in Egypt, gloating over his booty,

> *"Tidings out of the east and out of the north shall trouble him; and he shall go forth with great fury to destroy and utterly to sweep away many"* (Dan. 11:44).

What are these "tidings" that will so infuriate him? They are to come "out of the east and out of the north." "He shall go forth"—*to where?* We are not altogether in the dark. We return to Ezekiel's great prophecy once again:

> Verses 14-18. *"Therefore, son of man, prophesy, and say unto Gog, Thus saith the Lord Jehovah: In that day . . . thou shalt come from thy place out of the utmost parts of the north, thou, and many peoples with thee, all of them riding upon horses, a great company and a mighty*

*army; and thou shalt come up against My people Israel,
as a cloud to cover the land: . . . And it shall come to
pass in that day, when Gog shall come against the land
of Israel, saith the Lord Jehovah, that My wrath shall
come up into My nostrils."*

What are the "tidings" that will arouse the "fury" of the
Roman spoiler when in Egypt? What, unless he hears of the
mobilization of the cavalcades of Gog, ready to begin the fatal
march down past the cedars of Lebanon, on to the mountains
of Israel, thus thinking to take advantage of the Roman
Cæsar's troubles in Egypt and do a bit of pillaging for himself? Even so it is written: *"To take a spoil."* Nothing less
than "the middle [navel] of the earth" (v. 12) is the bacon
that lures the avaricious old grizzly out of his den in the north
parts.

But the "tidings" are also to be "out of the east." More
than "Persia," "Cush," "Put," and "Togarmah," in my humble
opinion, will be astir in "the east." A recent news item
furnishes a significant hint:

"TOKYO, Dec. 6 (Wednesday). (U.P.)—The popular
newspaper *Miyako* warned the United States today that if it
wants to avoid war with Japan the Washington government
must 'reconsider its attitude.'

"We wish to take this occasion frankly to tell the American
government and the American people that the people of Japan
until recently had thought that a Japanese-Russian understanding was unlikely and had believed that a Japanese-
American war was not possible.

"Now, however, Japanese sentiment toward Russia is much
more friendly."

"Impossible!" we hear someone say. "Impossible that
Fascist, Mikado-ruled Japan should ever enter into a non-
aggression pact and march with Bolshevik Russia!" However,
these are days when "impossible" things are being done. Only
a few days ago a non-aggression pact between Germany and
Russia was also "impossible." Things are becoming desperate
for Japan in China these days. Desperate men do desperate
things.

(NOTE:—Lo! As we are scanning the page proofs of these articles, press dispatches are informing us of a military alliance that has just been signed by Italy, Germany, and Japan! Verily, the desperate are indeed desperate! But it is only another temporary emergency alliance—another "Rome-Berlin Axis" affair that is foredoomed to disruption. Italy must drop out of that set-up. An alignment between Russia, Germany and Japan—strange bed-fellows as they may seem to be—would fit more perfectly into the prophetic chart. Verily, momentous hours are just ahead! And, in these desperate times, desperate men will continue to do desperate things! Euripides was right: "When a divinity would inflict evils on a man, he first strikes him mad!"

The Roman Conqueror Stirred to Fury.

Anyway, it is "out of the north, and out of the east," that the tidings shall come that will bring consternation to the Roman conqueror when in Egypt, and stir him to fury.

And when once the God of Israel is stirred to "fury" (v. 18), and the god of this world (Rev. 13:7, 8) also is stirred to "fury," and the "fury" of both is turned upon a common foe from "the north parts," there is only one conclusion to which we can come: the awful doom of Gog and his hordes, foretold by the prophets of Israel, will be at hand:

> Verses 21, 22. *"I will call for a sword against him* [Gog] *unto all My mountains, saith the Lord Jehovah: every man's sword shall be against his brother. And with pestilence and with blood will I enter into judgment with him; and I will rain upon him, and upon his hordes, and upon the many peoples that are with him, an overflowing shower, and great hailstones, fire, and brimstone."*

Let it be noted carefully that again it will be Jehovah Who will call for the sword. The ring will be in the nose of the Antichrist, and the chain will be in the hand of Israel's God! God's eternal purposes are to be carried out exactly to His own order! Howbeit, in this case the Antichrist will be quite willing to unsheathe his sword, for his "fury" against Gog will rage high! *"An overflowing shower, and great hailstones, fire, and brimstone"!* Call up Madrid, Warsaw, Rotterdam, or London, for information as to whether that is mere figurative language!

Europe's "man of the white horse," who is biding his time on the banks of the Tiber, is growing a bit feverish because of the meanderings of the Russian grizzly beyond his own lot. The present fever, sooner than we may think, may burn with "fury" *unrestrained.*

Benito Mussolini still possesses his famous "square jaw"! From a signed article in the *Evening Bulletin* (Philadelphia) we read:

"Il Duce of the protruding jaw hasn't budged an inch from the historic stand he took when he founded Fascism to combat Bolshevism in Italy at the end of the World War. *That jaw may be destined to become still more famous!"*

Just what will happen in Egypt when "tidings out of the north and out of the east" infuriate the new conqueror of Egypt? His blood, and the blood of the conquered "king of the south," doubtless will have been terribly spent. May this not be the opportune time for Gog to march unto the "spoil" in "the middle of the earth?" Conqueror and conquered in Egypt may then come to realize that *together* they must march, or the whole world will be devoured by the foe they both bitterly hate—the Berlin-Moscow monstrosity, out for no less a spoil than the world itself!

Israel's God Calls for a Sword.

As we have noted, the God of Israel will "call for a sword against him [Gog]" (v. 21). For what "sword" can God call in that day that will be powerful enough to meet the northern pillager of the land? The answer is not hard to find:

"*And the ten horns that thou sawest are ten kings, who have received no kingdom as yet; but they receive authority as kings, with the beast, for one hour. These have one mind, and they give their power and authority unto the beast. . . . For God did put in their hearts to do*

His mind, and to come to one mind, and to give their kingdom unto the beast, until the words of God should be accomplished" (Rev. 17:12, 13, 17, R. V.).

As said before, it is unthinkable that ten sovereign states will surrender their sovereignty into the hands of one man unless there is an absolutely compelling reason. The compelling reason will probably be the news "out of the east and out of the north."

The "ten kings," then in Egypt, will compose their differences, choose their leader, give him his temporary authority ("for one hour") to lead them. Then this mighty federated army—the revived Roman Empire in its final form—will take its orders from its imperial head, and go forth to meet the hordes of Gog on the plain of Esdraelon. The sword of the Antichrist (even as the sword of Nebuchadnezzar), paradoxical as it may seem, becomes the sword of the Lord God of Israel; and Gog and all his allies are cut to shreds there where "the stars in their courses fought against Sisera" (Judges 5:20), and where Gideon's "three hundred" routed the kings of the East. That ground has been soaked with blood more often than any other spot on earth. "Seven months shall the house of Israel be burying them . . . in the valley of Hamongog" (Ezek. 39:12, 15).

As for the head of the resurrected Roman Empire, even the Antichrist, this victory shall bring him to the zenith of his power, when all the world shall cry:

"Who is like unto the beast? and who is able to make war with him? . . . And power was given him over all kindreds, and tongues, and nations. And all that dwell upon the earth shall worship him" (Rev. 13:4, 7, 8).
"And he shall plant the tents of his palace between the seas in the glorious holy mountain; yet he shall come to his end, and none shall help him" (Dan. 11:45, R. V.).

How? We shall see!

VII

WHY PALESTINE WILL BE COVETED
BY THE NATIONS

THAT Palestine will be the prize for which the nations, in
the final hours of their dominion, will gamble their wealth
and their flesh and blood, must be a matter of knowledge to
all close students of the words spoken by the prophets of God.

When Palestine Will Be Trampled by the
Roman Conqueror.

It is into Palestine that the king who "shall do according to
his will" (Dan. 11:36) will march when the Almighty God
takes off his halter and permits him to go forth "conquering,
and to conquer" (Rev. 6:2). The words are clear and un-
mistakable: "He shall enter also into the glorious land . . .
And he shall plant the tabernacles of his palace between the
seas in the glorious holy mountain" (Dan. 11:41, 45). Palestine will become the possession of the Antichrist, "the man on
the white horse" who shall ride forth, as we have seen, from
Rome, headquarters of the revived Roman Empire. Only
Edom, Moab, and Ammon, the wilderness countries beyond
the Jordan, "shall escape out of his hand" (Dan. 11:41). The
reason for the escape of these three wilderness countries is
plain. God has ordained them to be a place of refuge for
Israel, when the Antichrist sets up his image (Rev. 13: 14,
15) "in the temple of God, shewing himself that he is God"
(2 Thess. 2:4). In that hour the "woman" (Israel) is to flee
"into the wilderness, where she hath a place prepared of God,
. . . where she is nourished for a time, and times, and half a
time [three and one-half years], from the face of the serpent"
(Rev. 12:6, 14). This is in harmony with our Lord's own
command, recorded in Matthew 24:15-18.

The head of the revived Roman Empire will not set covetous eyes on Abraham's land alone; for, after he has conquered

it in his last triumphant march—when he shall have marched on into Egypt where "the precious things of Egypt" (Dan. 11:43) shall have become his—Gog (Russia) and his hordes shall come forth from his "place out of the north parts" (Ezek. 38:15) "to take a spoil, and to take a prey . . . upon the people that are gathered out of the nations" (Ezek. 38:12). There can be no doubt about it, the Russian Bear, colossus of the north countries, will also covet the land given to Abraham and his seed for a possession forever. Inasmuch as all the nations of the earth, in the final hours of our age, will be allies of one or the other of these two colossuses, it can be truthfully said that Palestine will be a coveted prize for all nations. So much for the fact.

Why the Nations Covet Palestine.

But *why* will the nations covet this little strip of land? We know that again and again, through ages past, vast armies have fought and bled and died for its possession. The historian records nearly fifty separate blockades, sieges, captures, and destructions that Jerusalem has known. No land on earth has been so drenched with human blood. Its ruins have piled up until today they stand a literal fulfillment of an oft-repeated prophecy, *"And Jerusalem shall become heaps"* (Jer. 26:18; 9:11; Psa. 79:1; Micah 3:12, etc.).

Its Geographical Position.

Doubtless *one reason* why kings cast covetous eyes on this land is because of its strategic geographical position. Ezekiel declares it to be *"the navel of the earth"* (Ezek. 38:12, R.V., margin). Webster tells us that the *navel* is "the central part or point of anything." Elsewhere it is recorded: *"Thus saith the Lord God; This is Jerusalem: I have set it in the midst of the nations"* (Ezek. 5:5). Sir John Mandeville in his book of *Travels* wrote: "The Holy Land, which men call the land of promise or behest, passing all other lands, is *the most worthy land, most excellent, . . . the sovereign of all other lands . . . the heart and the middle of the world."* Pope Urban, Mohammed, and many others have declared that, because of its geographical position, Jerusalem is "placed in the very center of the world." Kurtz says: "Viewed geographically, politically, or commercially, Palestine is the *'umbilicus terrarum'* of the ancient world" (*His. Old Cov.*, Vol. 1, Page 147). Palestine—that vital link that connects the three mighty continents that carry on their bosoms the vast majority of mankind,—Asia, Europe, Africa! It marks the pathway over which the trade routes have run from the earliest story of our race. It will continue to be such to the end of time.

But in those days, when the knowledge of "what lies beyond" was exceedingly limited, how did those captive prophets know that Jerusalem was "the navel of the earth"? The only answer is—God! And that spot the All-wise chose as the place whereon His Son should sit enthroned when "out of Zion shall go forth the law, and the word of the Lord from Jerusalem" (Isa. 2:3); when "all the nations . . . shall even go up from year to year to worship the King" (Zech. 14:16).

Its Tremendous Natural Resources.

The *second reason* why Palestine will be coveted by the nations lies in its great natural wealth. As for the land itself, Dr. Clarke long ago disabused the mind of the world by telling it that the soil of that "desolate land" only needed water and cultivation to make it one of the most fertile areas on the face of the earth. The land is so rich that Mr. Malte Brun declared that near Bethlehem ripe peaches have been plucked on a tree grown from a seed planted the previous year. As many as five crops have been harvested off the same ground in a single year.

So fabulous as to be almost unbelievable is the value of the mineral salts in and about the Dead Sea, as that value is being estimated by chemists who are supposed to know. As soon as Jerusalem was captured in 1917 by General Allenby, a British geologist began to investigate the riches of the Dead Sea. Scientists have in hand a detailed report of the various minerals, and also the extent and the value of them. We are now informed that in that desolate spot there lie embedded from twelve hundred billions to thirteen hundred billions of dollars worth of recoverable salts. We are told that there is two hundred and sixty million dollars' worth of bromine, so useful for medical purposes; of potash there is seventy billions of dollars' worth; and of magnesium chloride eight hundred twenty-five billions' of dollars worth, and vast values of other minerals. We are told that the wealth that lies embosomed in the earth at that point is worth more than all the known gold that has been dug from the bowels of all the earth. What these minerals may mean to the world, especially in that prophetic day when, we are told, the deserts shall blossom as a rose, is indicated in the fact that they are already making the gardens in the neighborhood of the sea itself productive almost beyond the wildest dreams of men.

In a recent editorial in the *Los Angeles Times* we were assured that "Gardens of workers on the banks [of the Dead Sea] grow beans two feet long and radishes as big as a policeman's shillalah—and oranges that weigh a pound." Little wonder that the most recent edition of the *Encyclopædia Britannica* assures us that "the future of this, the most interesting of all seas, will be watched with interest whilst modern enterprise takes a hesitating step towards the fulfillment of Ezekiel's prophetic vision."

For centuries upon centuries it has been called the Dead Sea, yet it is just like our God to make life spring forth from the dead. From that desolation will come the fertilizer that will make the deserts of the earth blossom as a rose. In more ways than one life bursts forth from Judea.

Verily, the fulfillment of Ezekiel's great prophecy is on the way:

"And the desolate land shall be tilled, whereas it lay desolate in the sight of all that passed by. And they shall say, This land that was desolate is become like the garden of Eden; and the waste and desolate and ruined cities are become fenced, and are inhabited. Then the heathen that are left round about you shall know that I the Lord build the ruined places, and plant that that was desolate: I the Lord have spoken it, and I will do it" (Ezek. 36:34-36).

Moses, approaching his departure from this world, imparted his blessing upon the twelve tribes. "Of Zebulun he said, Rejoice, Zebulun, . . . for they shall suck of the abundance of the seas, and of treasures hid in the sand" (Deut. 33:18, 19). Our Lord declared: "Verily I say unto you, Till heaven and earth pass away, one jot or one tittle shall in no wise pass away from the law, till all things be accomplished" (Matt. 5:18, R.V.). Therefore, Zebulun *must* "suck of the abundance of the seas, and of treasures hid in the sand."

What can these words mean? Look on your map showing the division of the land among the tribes. There is Zebulun, a very small part of the land, located on the sea, just above Mt. Carmel. But on that short stretch of seashore is modern Haifa. And Haifa very recently has emerged as one of the great harbors of the world. Thus we are witnessing a remarkable fulfillment of the prophecy of Jacob, uttered over thirty-six centuries ago: *"Zebulun shall dwell at the haven of the sea; and he shall be for an haven of ships"* (Gen. 49:13).

The business sagacity of world Jewry is rapidly developing this harbor, and its trade facilities are literally sucking into it "the abundance of the seas." A great pipe line more than six hundred miles in length, from Bagdad to Haifa, is literally sucking vast quantities of oil out of the sands of Iraq, and pouring it into the holds of the great ships that are carrying it to the nations of the earth. This oily highway alone is enough to make Palestine a land coveted by the kings of the earth. Verily, the riches are fast accumulating in Palestine that shall cause Gog, even Russia, "the king of the north," to "think an evil thought: and . . . say, I will go up to the land of unwalled villages . . . to take a spoil . . . and upon the people that are gathered out of the nations, which have gotten cattle and goods, that dwell in the midst of the land [i.e., the navel of the earth]" (Ezek. 38:10-12).

Its Throne Will Govern the Nations.

There is still *another reason* why the nations of the earth are casting covetous eyes on Abraham's land. Once upon a time the great Napoleon, an exile on St. Helena, spread a map before some of his friends. On this map the British Isles were colored red. The little Corsican placed his finger on that red spot and said: "Gentlemen, had it not been for that red spot, I would have conquered the world!" The reddest spot on the world's map today is Palestine—reddened not only by the blood of countless hordes of humanity, but by the precious blood of the Son of God Himself. It is not unthinkable that Satan should gather together the master-minds over which he rules, spread before them the map of the nations, lay his finger on that reddest of spots, and say: "If we can conquer and rule that red spot, we can rule the world!"

We must give the master-mind of all the dominions that are anti-God, credit for being able to read the Scriptures. He knows well that it is written: "Sing and rejoice, O daughter of Zion: for, lo, I come, and I will dwell in the midst of thee, saith the Lord. And many nations shall be joined to the Lord in that day, and shall be My people: and I will dwell in the midst of thee, . . . and the Lord shall inherit Judah his portion in the holy land, and shall choose Jerusalem" (Zech. 2:10-12). He knows that the Lord of hosts has decreed that though "the kings of the earth set themselves, and the rulers take counsel together, against the Lord, and against His anointed . . . yet have I set My king upon My holy hill of Zion" (Psa. 2:2, 6).

It is Jerusalem that the anti-God forces of Satan and all his puppet kings must conquer and hold, if he is to continue his bloody reign over the nations of the earth. Therefore, "he shall plant the tabernacles of his palace between the seas in the glorious holy mountain" (Dan. 11:45). In a word, Satan and his cohorts are going to try to beat our Lord to the throne in Palestine. It will be Satan's last desperate attempt in this age. We are not surprised, therefore, to see Palestine outstanding in the world's news today, with the eyes of all kings in her direction.

The purposes of the Devil have been declared: "I will exalt my throne above the stars of God. . . . I will ascend above the heights of the clouds; I will be like the most High" (Isa. 14:13, 14). His audacity knows no bounds. Once upon a time he even invited the incarnate God to fall down upon His knees and worship him! (See Luke 4:7.)

Whether we like to believe it or not, Satan is "the prince of this world" (John 14:30). "All the kingdoms of the world . . . and the glory of them" (Luke 4:5, 6) are his. These kingdoms and the glory of them will never be delivered up without a battle. Therefore, in their audacity and self-deception "the kings of the earth, and their armies [will be] gathered together to make war against Him [the Christ] that sat on the horse, and against His army" (Rev. 19:19). All nations will gather together against Jerusalem to battle (Zech. 12:2, 3; 14:2; Joel 3:2; Zeph. 3:8). The last fight to which the nations will march in this age will be, therefore, for the possession of the city of David and the land of Palestine. From that march they will never return. On that battlefield the buzzards shall gather for a royal banquet upon the carcasses of kings. Then the very stars in the heavens will rock to and fro before the tumultuous vibrations of "great voices in heaven, saying, The kingdoms of this world are become the kingdoms of our Lord, and of His Christ; and He shall reign for ever and ever. . . . We give Thee thanks, O Lord God Almighty, . . . because Thou hast taken to Thee Thy great power, and hast reigned!" (Rev. 11:15, 17.)

VIII

HERBERT HOOVER'S VISION OF "THE NEW CAVALRY"

Herbert Hoover Becomes a Prophet.

HARD-HEADED, clear-visioned, practical men of affairs, who have been out of their caps and gowns long enough to enable them to do straight thinking, are beginning to realize that this old world has made a sad mistake in making a mock of sin, and forgetting the God of the Bible. No less a personage than an ex-President of the United States, a man

who, in the course of his lifetime, has touched the world of bitter realities as few men have touched it, recently spoke as
would a prophet of God, before the Overseas Press Club of New
York. Next morning, the newspapers of the nation gave us
a digest of that address, as follows:

*"Hoover made no mention of either Hitler or Stalin in his
address, but there was no mistaking his reference to Nazi and
Soviet doctrines when he declared the Four Horsemen of the
Apocalypse have today been increased to nine, and listed
'the new cavalry':*
'Imperialism, the destroyer of the independence of nations;
'Intolerance, the destroyer of minorities;
'Statism, the destroyer of personal liberty;
'Atheism, the destroyer of faith;
'Hate, the destroyer of the unity of mankind.
*'After these ride war and death. And finally there sweep
famine and pestilence . . .*
*'These destroyers will profoundly affect American life even
if they do not visit our own shores.' "*

These words came from the lips of one who but a few short
years ago stood at the helm of one of the most powerful Ships
of State in all the world, a man who is still one of the world's
most trusted advisers. Thus, one of the world's most far-
sighted statesmen sees as the prophets saw, the estate in which
the Gentile colossuses and all their satellites find themselves at
the evening of man's days—six thousand years (*Cf.* 2 Pet.
3:8)—upon this earth. Let us consider this statesman's
marvelous condensation of the world's outstanding trends,
which fit so perfectly into the mold of the great prophecies that
describe world conditions as they must be when the sands of
man's day run low.

Former President Hoover has summed up the situation in a
way that largely agrees with the prophecies of the "holy men
of God [who] spake as they were moved by the Holy Ghost"
(2 Pet. 1:21). However, he declared (as reported) that "the
task of re-establishing civilization in Europe will rest with the
United States." If, within his idea of "civilization," there is
cessation of "wars and rumors of wars," followed by peace, con-

tentment, righteousness, and justice, then the task can never rest with a State that within itself is growing less and less law-abiding, and more and more apostate, morally and spiritually, with each tick of the clock. The civilization that is worth while awaits the return of the Son of God from the heavens!

Nine Horsemen Now.

Mr. Hoover had previously expressed his conviction, as we recall, that the "Four Horsemen of the Apocalypse" are riding today in their saddles. Now he insists that they have been joined by five other, and that nine "horsemen" now ride. Whether Mr. Hoover realizes it or not, the five he names are all Biblical horsemen who are to ride the pathways of the earth in the van of the famous four. And all nine are to ride together to battle, and to their doom against the great white charger whereon shall be seated "The Word of God," "Faithful and True," "KING OF KINGS, AND LORD OF LORDS" (Rev. 19:11-16). If Mr. Hoover has appraised our generation aright, can any true believer in a covenant-keeping God fail of the conviction that man's six days (6,000 years) are drawing to a close in gigantic failure, and that the Lord's day is at hand?

The first horseman in the line of "the new cavalry" is named by Mr. Hoover:

"IMPERIALISM: *The destroyer of the independence of nations.*"

Exactly that horseman, according to all the prophets, is to ride. The lexicographer will tell you that imperialism is the centralization of power or governmental authority into the hands of one man—an emperor, czar, or dictator. Exactly that shall be in the dusk of man's day. It is written:

"And I stood upon the sand of the sea, and saw a beast rise up out of the sea, having seven heads and ten horns, and upon his horns ten crowns . . . and the dragon gave him his power, and his seat, and great authority . . . and power was given him over all kindreds, and tongues, and nations" (Rev. 13:1, 2, 7).

Utterly blind is that man who cannot see that within the last score of years a world, supposedly "safe for democracy," has rushed with incredible speed into the arms of imperialism. Even the democracies, so-called, on one pretext or another, have more or less resigned themselves into the arms of some pretended saviour from human ill.

Mr. Hoover names the second horseman:

"INTOLERANCE: *The destroyer of minorities.*"

And that horseman also is galloping over the earth. His foul breath pollutes the sanctuaries of the Church as well as of the State. But it is written:

"Know this, that in the last days . . . all that would live godly in Christ Jesus shall suffer persecution" (2 Tim. 3:1, 12).

"And I beheld another beast coming up out of the earth; . . . and he had power to . . . cause that as many as would not worship the image of the beast should be killed. And he causeth all, both small and great, rich and poor, free and bond, to receive a mark in their right hand, or in their foreheads; and that no man might buy or sell, save he that had the mark, or the name of the beast, or the number of his name" (Rev. 13:11-17).

Yes, the horseman, Intolerance, rides. The Jew knows it well. Christians in German, Russian, and Italian concentration camps also can testify. In fact, political and religious minorities everywhere likewise can testify.

The third horseman in this "new cavalry" is named:

"STATISM: *The destroyer of personal liberty.*"

When the State sets itself up to possess the bodies and the souls of men, that is *Statism,* or *Statolatry.* As it was at the first advent of our Lord, even thus shall it be at His second advent—Rome, the State, was worshiped as the supreme deity. To the temple of Capitoline Jupiter marched the worshiper of Rome, with his thank-offerings. And the Christians who refused to march died by the tens of thousands!

As the Seer of Patmos scanned the vistas of twenty centuries ahead, he saw them dying again, *"slain for the word of God, and for the testimony which they held"* (Rev. 6:9). "Nebuchadnezzar," the State, will again erect the image of a world religion; and as the Seer beheld, "It was given unto him to make war with the saints" (Rev. 13:7). Once again the imperialistic decree will be heard in the earth: "If ye worship not, ye shall be cast . . . into the midst of a burning fiery furnace; and who is that God that shall deliver you out of my hands?" (Dan. 3:15.)

The Church having been "caught up" (1 Thess. 4:17), the "saints" will then be of the children of Israel who have been turned away from their idols by the testimony of "two witnesses" (Rev. 11:3), one of whom will be Elijah (Mal. 4:5, 6), and the other, Enoch or Moses. Then, when they "shall see the abomination of desolation" (Matt. 24:15) set up for their worship, they shall refuse to bow the knee. "Then shall be great tribulation, such as was not since the beginning of the world to this time, no, nor ever shall be" (Matt. 24:21). And when Israel is in the furnace of her greatest tribulation, then once again the Son of God shall be seen "walking in the midst of the fire" (Dan. 3:25), even as He walked in Nebuchadnezzar's furnace. Verily, "the Lord will be the hope of His people" (Joel 3:16).

The fourth personage riding in "the new cavalry" is named:

"ATHEISM: *The destroyer of faith.*"

The "sure word of prophecy" even so declares. "When the Son of man cometh, shall He find faith on the earth?" (Luke 18:8.) "Now the Spirit speaketh expressly, that in the latter times some shall depart from the faith, giving heed to seducing spirits, and doctrines of devils" (1 Tim. 4:1). "This know also, that in the last days perilous times shall come. For men shall be . . . lovers of pleasure more than lovers of God" (2 Tim. 3:1, 2, 4). "For the time will come when they will not endure sound doctrine" (2 Tim. 4:3). "That day [the day of Christ] shall not come, except there come a falling away first, and that man of sin be revealed, the son of perdition" (2 Thess. 2:3).

The Antichrist will deify himself. "And all that dwell upon

the earth shall worship him, whose names are not written in the book of life" (Rev. 13:8). Thus the world will turn to atheism, and worship an atheist as its god. Ex-President Hoover says: "We are on the way!" Communism, Socialism, Fascism—atheistic or of atheistic tendencies—one and all are sweeping on over the whole world. Colleges, universities, and even church seminaries are everywhere more and more being permeated with the leaven of damnation—atheism!

The fifth of the riders in "the new cavalry" is named:

"HATE: *The destroyer of the unity of mankind.*"

A great twentieth century statesman becomes conscious of the fact that we are witnessing a positive fulfillment of the Master's first century prophecy: *"And ye shall be hated of all nations for My name's sake. And then shall many be offended, and shall betray one another, and shall hate one another"* (Matt. 24:9, 10).

It is a war-torn world. War is the product of hate. Glance about over this world of men. Behold, how the Gentile hates the Jew, and the Jew hates the Gentile! How the Moslem hates the Christian, and the Christian hates the Moslem! How the Fascist hates the Communist, and the Communist hates the Fascist! How the Englishman hates the German, and the German hates the Englishman! How the Jap hates the Russian! And how the Russian hates everybody! Poor old hate-torn earth! Yes, the fifth horseman rides!

Can anyone doubt that these horsemen are to be followed *immediately* by the famous four of Revelation 6? Imperialism, Intolerance, Statism, Atheism, and Hate—what could possibly follow these spirits of the Antichrist but the Antichrist himself, astride his own "white horse"? (Rev. 6:1, 2.) And who can follow the Antichrist riding over the earth with these spirits of his but the rider of the red horse—War? And who but the rider of the black horse—Famine—has ever followed in the wake of war? And who but *Death,* the rider of the pale horse, has ever followed famine?

And who but the rider of that great white horse that will ride forth from the opened heavens, the hope of the ages, can follow death? Death—and *then*, Death's conqueror! For, "the last enemy that shall be destroyed is death" (1 Cor. 15:26).

After war, peace! After death, life! After the cross, the crown! After the tears, the joy! After the parting, the meeting! After the Devil, the Christ! Then let "the new cavalry" ride! Let "the old cavalry" come! The Victor and the victory draw nigh!

IX

THE "BEASTS" AND THE WORLD'S GREATEST MASSACRE

A FEW rods from where I write this chapter, "Old Faithful," the giant geyser of The Yellowstone, has just completed her hourly task. She has just sprayed the morning sunlight with many thousands of gallons of liquid crystal, puffing far up into the air her great white clouds of glory.

About one hour hence the watchers will gather again to behold this marvel of nature thrust forth from the deep, dark bowels of the earth this same overflowing splendor. But what assurance have these watchers who shall gather here from every corner of the earth one hour hence that they are not going to be sadly disappointed? This is their assurance: *Never within the memory of man has this geyser failed in the performance of its hourly task!* That is the reason why she is known to every lover of nature as—*"Old Faithful."*

Another "Old Faithful."

Besides me as I write, is another "Old Faithful"—my precious Bible! And why call it "Old Faithful"? Because never once within the memory of any who have lived on this earth has it disappointed the watchers on Zion's walls! In due time, to its minutest detail, every event that it promised has come to pass. That is the reason why, all over the earth, the believing children of God are gathering around its sacred pages in these tumultuous times in all confidence. They know that soon there is to be a burst of glory that shall fill heaven and earth with splendor—the splendor of "the glorious appearing of our great God and our Saviour Jesus Christ" (Titus 2:13).

Twenty centuries ago, the world had reached a starless midnight. But there were a few who watched for the appearing of the promised "star in the east" (Matt. 2:2) that was to pierce the darkness of that midnight. There was Simeon, who had grown old "waiting for the consolation of Israel" (Luke 2:25). Not one moment late, the "star in the east" appeared in the heavens; and, Mary laid in the arms of old Simeon, "the consolation of Israel . . . a light to lighten the Gentiles, and the glory of Thy people, Israel" (Luke 2:25, 32). They who now faithfully watch, like Daniel (9:2), may understand "by books" that again the "Star"—"the consolation of Israel"—is about to appear. And, though to impatient watchers, He may appear to "tarry" (Matt. 24:48; 25:5), yet not one moment late the "Star" will shine forth, and "they shall see the Son of man coming in the clouds of heaven with power and great glory" (Matt. 24:30).

"Deutschland Uber Alles!"—A Dream.

This is the cry that comes ever and anon from the German "Fool's Paradise." We heard the same exultant cry a quarter of a century ago. That cry in all Teutonic lands expresses "the mind's eternal heaven." One exiled Kaiser knows that it is "such stuff as dreams are made on." I knew twenty-five years ago that it was only a dream. Again, I know it is *now*. My "Old Faithful" before me reveals no reality in that dream!

And, with this backing from "Old Faithful," I shall not hesitate to make a statement that, *as I write*, seems so contrary to the existing course of events—I assert that Adolf Hitler is a dreamer, and all his enslaved puppets who dream together with their master, are due, in time, for a rude awakening! A satanic kingdom *is* to arise within the permissive will of God that will be for "one hour" (Rev. 17:12) "uber alles"

Rev. 13:7); but, as we have before pointed out, it will not be a kingdom *north* of the Rhine, nor will it be a one-kingdom affair. It will be an allied kingdom, sponsored by ten sorely tried kings, who will seek to save themselves from some gigantic enemy by the centralization of all their own power, armies, and fleets, for "one hour" in the hands of "the beast"; and, "the beast" does not emerge from any Teutonic or Muscovite den.

The German dictators have said over and over in their communiqués, as the god of war seemed to smile upon them, *"All is proceeding according to plan!"* I have agreed with them. But—according to *whose* plan? It is said that Alexander the Great, when he marched his swift-moving columns into Palestine, entered the Temple in Jerusalem. While there, the high priest showed him the scroll of the prophet Daniel. Alexander was greatly interested in discovering that his own plans, as he thought they were, were the plans of the God of Israel, and were all written down by Daniel before he (Alexander) was born!

If the tyrant of Berlin were not so blinded in his hate of the Jew, and of the "Jews' 'Book,'" and would only refer to its pages, he might gain wisdom in the discovery that he, and all his contemporaneous ilk, are following plans written down by Jews more than two thousand years before he opened his eyes to the light of day in the home of Alois Schicklgruber, a pompous inspector of customs on the Austrian-Bavarian frontier. (Schicklgruber, an illegitimate son of a peasant girl, took his father's name, Hitler, when he married Adolf's mother). Daniel and Ezekiel would reveal to this German Frankenstein that he, and such as he, are only cogs on the wheels of God's own eternal "plans" that are rolling on for the fulfillment of every divine purpose in Christ as perfectly as the stars roll on in their courses through the heavens above. All the machinations of these godless dictators were known to the Jews two and three thousand years ago. Yes, "Old Faithful" reveals them all!

Already, we are hearing the deep growl of the old Bear, glowering deep back within his den in "the north parts." That is as it should be. (*Cf.* Ezek. 38:15). Already it is being intimated that there is a real strain on "the Berlin-Rome Axis," even though the "axis" still *seems* to be operating in splendid fashion. That is as it should be. (*Cf.* Dan. 11:23). Already there is a man on a white horse, ready to ride from Rome. That is as it should be. (*Cf.* Rev. 6:1, 2). Already, there is a man on a red horse, taking peace from the earth. That is as it should be. (*Cf.* Rev. 6:4). Already, far-sighted statesmen are pointing out (even if the false prophets in our pulpits refuse to do so) the riding of the black horse in the distance. (*Cf.* Rev. 6:5, 6). To this we shall refer later.

At this point, we wish to state again very clearly that *we are not proclaiming that Benito Mussolini is the Antichrist.* We have before pointed out that prior to the rapture of the saints to meet the Lord in the air, no man can be pointed out as the Antichrist with any degree of certainty. Mussolini might pass off the stage. What about his successor? We are not saying that Adolf Hitler is positively the rider on the "red horse" in Revelation 6. We are not saying that the famine of next winter, if it comes, will be a fulfillment of the riding forth of "a black horse" in Rev. 6:5, 6. *But we are saying that if the mighty God who rules over all has set the present hour for drawing man's day to a close, the forces are now operating in the world for the fulfillment of the prophetic picture with marvelous exactness.*

"The Greatest Massacre Ever Witnessed."

The Sunday School Times (Feb. 24, 1940) quotes from a letter to its editors, written by "a keen observer in Europe," as follows:

"Israel and the nations are guilty. They have gone their own way. Idolatry has been the rule, pride the motive. The war that is being waged now is God's warning,—perhaps the last,—before the universal outpouring of the vials of His wrath. It is as if the Lord were pleading for the last time with a world at large and especially with His people to give Him the lordship which is His right. It does not take more than a cursory reading of the news concerning the European situation to show the student of the 'more sure word of prophecy' that the Lord is preparing the world for the final battle of this age. In spite of all official neutrality, Europe is divided into two camps, so far as sympathies are concerned. . . . *The scene is being prepared for the greatest massacre that the world has ever witnessed.*"

That was written only four short months ago. Already "the greatest massacre ever witnessed" is on! Gigantic fortresses on wheels dash forward, hurling destruction, desolation, and death over the earth. Giant planes drop bombs from high up in the heavens on old men, women, and cradled babies. It is not war—it is horrible massacre! Finland, Norway, Holland, Belgium, and France have just witnessed massacres unparalleled in the records of men. The Nazi brute, unchained, gloats gleefully as he tells the world that he expects soon to turn the British Isles into a charnel house "the like of which the world has never seen." The "beasts" are literally slobbering at the mouth, smacking their gory lips at the prospect of filling up their chalices once again with the red wine that they know must gurgle, in part, from the fluttering hearts of tender, milk-fed babes. If this old world is not soon converted into a sadistic hell, it is not going to be the fault of the totalitarian hellcats that now roam Europe.

"Beasts" in the Form of Men.

"Beasts"? If the Spirit of God, author of Holy Writ, designated Nebuchadnezzar, Cyrus, Alexander, and Cæsar, as "four great beasts" (Dan. 7:3), then what must we call this modern triumvirate—Mussolini, Stalin, and Hitler? For many years, our modernistic intelligentsia, capped and gowned, *or surpliced*, has amused itself with self-flattery, spending most of its time in boasting of man's high attainments upon the earth, his high degree of civilization, his great advancement over the "horse-and-buggy" days of our fathers—in general, telling us all how good we have come to be! When we pointed out to them the Biblical prophecies of coming human failure and consequent judgments, especially as written in the Book of The Revelation, they ridiculed all literal interpretation of those prophecies as "old witches' tales." "Utterly impossible of any literal fulfilment in this enlightened age," they cried. They gave no credence whatever to the idea that our age would draw to a close with the riding forth of the four horsemen with "power given unto them over the fourth part of the earth, to kill with the sword, and with hunger, and with death, and with the beasts of the earth"(Rev. 6:8). But these intellectuals are talking in whispers—whispers of fear—*now!*

The writer used to think that these "beasts of the earth" that come in the wake of famine would be beasts that would prowl forth, hunger-driven, from the forests of the earth, even as the she-bears prowled forth "out of the wood" (II Kings 2:24) and destroyed the mockers in the days of Elisha. And it may be so. However, has not God Himself portrayed the Gentile dictators of the earth as "beasts"? If all the records of men are to be believed, "beasts" they are, and as "beasts" they kill! We are doing no violence to a proper interpretation of the Scripture in believing that the "beasts" the great Revelator saw in his vision prowled not forth before his astonished vision from the forested mountain fastnesses of the earth, but rather from the great cosmopolitan centers of the earth; and, by them, shall "the fourth part of the earth" be killed.

Ex-President Hoover still more recently has warned the world that it is even now face to face with the specter of "the most disastrous famine in history"—a famine, he declared, that would bring suffering and death unparalleled in the annals of men. British statesmen are likewise issuing this same warning. Reports are in the air that Germany's rulers are beginning to have a haunting fear, and that they are knocking at the doors of the food stores of the earth, offering to barter almost anything they possess, for food supplies on ahead. Bread, not bullets, may yet upset the German's dream of world dominion. Unless Germany can find a way to command the seas to bring food supplies into her ports, she soon may find her chickens coming home to roost.

The "Stuff" That Failed.

For many years past, we have been hearing unregenerate teachers and preachers proclaiming:

> "We men of earth here have the stuff
> Of Paradise—we have enough!
> We need no other thing to build
> The stairs into the Unfulfilled—
> No other ivory for the doors—
> No other marble for the floors—
> No other cedar for the beam
> And dome of man's immortal dream.
>
> Here on the paths of every day—
> Here on the common human way
> Is all the stuff the gods would take
> To build a Heaven, to mold and make
> New Edens. Ours is the stuff sublime
> To build Eternity in time!"

When the God of the heavens heard men sing that song,— well, is it not written: "He that sitteth in the heavens shall laugh" (Ps. 2:4)? He certainly laughs *now!* And, these builders of "Eternity in time" now squat all over Europe beside whatsoever "stuff" the Mussolini-Stalin-Hitler Juggernaut is leaving to them, whispering with Lord Byron: "A change came o'er the spirit of my dream!"

The Utterly Beastly Nature of European Dictators Should Be Known.

The bald facts are that the deeds of the totalitarian "assassinocrats" of Europe are such that the dust that for ages has lain cold and gray in the tombs of Pharaoh, Epiphanes, Herod, Nero, Caligula, Attila, and Genghis Khan must be turning green with envy! Mussolini's brutality used in gaining absolute power over every foe he might have had in Italy is a matter of history. The barbaric cruelties practiced on his island prisons in the Mediterranean have horrified the world. Senator Reed of Missouri, a few years ago, from the floor of the Senate did not hesitate to brand Mussolini as "the most dangerous man now living, the man who has the cruelty of Caligula, the monstrous egotism of Nero, who possesses the soul of a monster who would again set the fires of war to sweep the world."

As for Joseph Stalin, no more beastly creature ever ruled over man. If any ruler in history ever equaled him, it is certain that none ever surpassed him. The Georgian hyena literally loves the odor of rotting corpses. Several years ago, when the enslaved and over-taxed farmers in Russia protested that they would not raise food beyond their own needs if they had to drag chains with them as they walked the furrows, Stalin sent his daggered agents among these farmers, and took away from them every particle of food upon which he could lay his hands, and left them to starve. It was the first great famine, deliberately planned and carried out, by a beast in human form. Men and women quickly shrank to whitened skeletons; little children pulled at their mothers' skirts and begged piteously for *"Food! Food!"*, and babes sucked blood instead of milk from their mothers' breasts. As they starved, Stalin sat back and grinned in the supreme satisfaction that belongs only to a hyena awaiting its meal of rot. Between five and six million of his own subjects died of starvation.

As if that were not sufficient for his vengeance, he then sent into the famine-swept district, the dreaded OGPU, and arrested 750,000 kulaks, who were suspected of being out of sympathy with his deeds. And since no trials were allowed, each "arrest" was practically a death warrant. Then began the daily executions, without a chance for defense, and without mercy. Hundreds disappeared daily, dying in ways too horrible for description. Agonies unspeakable in concentration camps, which were surrounded by wires highly charged with electricity and manned by the lowest types of human scum; horrors within the frozen fastnesses of Siberia into which hundreds of thousands were driven, never to return— these are samples of his planned cruelties.

If I shall appear to exaggerate when I say that authentic reports as to what transpired continually in Stalin's torture chambers would make Nero's torture chambers seem places of bliss beside them, I have to relate but one example.

Imagine, if you can stretch your imagination that far without going mad yourself—imagine a superheated chamber—the *parilka*—into which men and women were packed so densely that when one fainted, he still stood erect on his swollen and benumbed feet. And then, shut off from all ventilation, the poisoned atmosphere was heated more and more by steam, until men and women tore their clothing from their bodies in fighting the heat; and then were attacked by swarms of vermin seeking blood! If that can be surpassed in all the annals of cruelty, I haven't read it yet. And to think that in this "advanced age," in this "twentieth century," a man like that should be left to live, and rule with iron hand over 180,-000,000 slaves! It seems incredible, but it is true!

In Berlin dwells the third of the three powerful "beasts" that have overrun Europe, and bid fair to overrun the world—*der Fuehrer* (the Leader) to 80,000,000 more enslaved puppets. As he reigns, at his right hand sits Herman Goering, dope fiend and ex-inmate of an insane asylum,—Hitler's "Minister without Portfolio." At his left hand sits Josef Goebbels, a neurotic sex-crazed journalist—Hitler's "Minister of Propaganda," *i.e.*, Hitler's "Minister of Lies." These three rabid Jew-baiters are out-smarted in their fiendishness only by Joseph Stalin. I shall not weary my readers by recounting the horrors of their deeds. They have often been told to the world, and told by sources of information whose reliability is beyond question.

Why have I recalled these scenes of horror? For only one reason: to give an answer to the oft repeated assertion by the critics that "such things as we read in the Book of the Revelation are impossible of a literal fulfillment in this enlightened age"! It is time men and women are aroused to the fact that this world has arrived at a place where it is desperately in need of a Savior—of the One Who is to come from above. It is to set forth the good and sufficient reasons why the Lord God of Israel is soon to unleash the thunderbolts of His wrath upon an unregenerate world.

"The Darkest Hour in the World's History"?
Yes—and, No!

Time and again the press recently, has brought to us statements from the trampled nations of Europe, describing the present time as "the darkest hour in the world's history." It would not seem to be an exaggerated statement. However, it need not be so dark as it would appear. The eye of faith pierces the darkest cloud and sees just above it the Conqueror of Death and the Destroyer of Oppressors! "When these things begin to come to pass, then look up, and lift up your heads; for your redemption draweth nigh" (Luke 21:28). His great white charger is champing at his bits! The foot of the Lord of Glory is in the stirrup! "The beasts of the earth" have brought death! But their reign shall be exceeding short! "The Lord will be the hope of His people" (Joel 3:16). As for the "beasts," our Lord "shall break them with a rod of iron . . . shalt dash them in pieces like a potter's vessel" (Ps. 2:9).

"I have seen the wicked in great power, and spreading himself like a green bay tree. Yet he passed away, and, lo, he was not: I sought him, but he could not be found" (Ps. 37:35, 36).

"OLD FAITHFUL" WILL NOT FAIL!

X

"AND THERE SHALL BE EARTHQUAKES"

THE story of man's sojourn upon the earth, from its beginning, compels the belief that when sin plays havoc with the spiritual man, nature plays havoc with the physical man. That much defined, indefinable something that seems to embrace everything but God—that something which we call *nature*—is assuredly something that must be subject to, and respond to, the perfect will of God. Otherwise, nature, and not God, would be omnipotent in the universe. Nature is simply God at work. It is, therefore, only to be expected that when the iniquities of men become great and the holiness of God is violated, nature will render her protest.

When the Earth Became a Waste.

The Scriptures lead us to believe that there first existed on this earth a pre-Adamic race, and that that race departed far from the holiness of God and brought down upon itself swift judgment. It is written of the earth that, originally, God "created it *not a waste*" (Isa. 45:18, R. V.). It was created "standing out of the water and in the water . . . [and] the world that then was, being overflowed with water, perished" (2 Peter 3:5, 6). Thus, "the earth became a waste and empty" (literal translation of Gen. 1:2). "And darkness was upon the face of the deep." Then, in re-creation, "the Spirit of God moved upon the face of the waters. . . . And God said, Let the waters . . . be gathered together unto one place, and let the dry land appear" (Gen. 1:2, 9). Then, once again, as now, the earth was seen "standing out of the water and in the water." Only some vast and mighty convulsion of nature could ever have brought about that first terrible retribution upon the earth.

Then, upon the resurrected earth, the parents of our race disobeyed the laws of God. Nature immediately retaliated by thrusting up from the bosom of the earth the thorns and the thistles; and, "the whole creation groaneth and travaileth in pain together until now" (Rom. 8:22).

Some sixteen or seventeen centuries after the tragedy in Eden, "God looked upon the earth, and, behold, . . . all flesh had corrupted His way upon the earth" (Gen. 6:12). Once again nature responded to its God, and "all the fountains of the great deep [were] broken up" (Gen. 7:11). The waters that all but swept the human race from the face of the earth did not all pour forth from the opened "windows of heaven." The sea sighed with her God, lifted her great bosom, and the waters rolled out over the land to mingle with the waters that fell from the heavens. Again nature avenged man's disrespect and contempt for the righteousness of God.

Prosperity—and Forgetting God.

Less than five centuries later, Sodom and Gomorrah became the great centers of civilization. It is an old, old story. With the riches, the glory, and the boasted "advancement" of those cities, they forgot God, and became also centers of corruption. Again nature aroused. The eminent geologist, Professor Emerson, as quoted by M. G. Kyle in *The Deciding Voice of the Monuments* (page 67), declares that beneath that mass of iniquity there was a "sinking of the ground, at the time when geology and history join, which, with its earthquakes, overthrew the cities of the Plain and caused the outpour of petroleum from the many fault-fissures and the escape of great volumes of sulphurous and gaseous emanation, which, ignited . . . furnished the brimstone and fire from heaven, and the smoke of the land going up as the smoke of a furnace which Abraham saw from the plains of Judea." Again nature saw to it that "vice received her retribution due."

When Egypt arose to power and glory, and led the world in the fine arts of civilization, she also became a sink of iniquity. Again nature responded to her God and exacted her penalties. The rivers of Egypt turned to rotting rivers of blood. The dust of her streets turned to creeping vermin. Murrain destroyed her cattle. Lightning, rain, and hail, "very grievous," beat down upon man and beast, "smote every herb . . . and brake every tree of the field." And a pall of "thick darkness," "even darkness which may be felt," terrified the land.

Uzziah, king of Judah, his heart lifted up with pride, very grievously trespassed against the law of Jehovah. Spurning the solemn protests of Azariah, the high priest, and of eighty other priests of God, he assumed priestly prerogatives that never could be his, and burned incense upon the golden altar in the temple of God. Then an earthquake struck, so great that the very memory of it made it a point from which to reckon time in Israel (Amos 1:1). It was also cited as an example of similar terrible judgments that are yet to fall upon the earth at the close of man's day (Zech. 14:5).

Nature Mourns at the Crucifixion.

When Satan-directed despisers of God descended to the depths where they vented their spleen by spitting upon the Lord of Glory, scourging Him, and nailing Him to a tree, nature again expressed her protest, for, "the earth did quake, and the rocks rent" (Matt. 27:51). The very sun hid its face from the awfulness of man's iniquity, and "there was darkness over all the earth" (Luke 23:44).

The ancient story of man is replete with evidence that when he departs from fellowship with God, nature works disastrously upon his habitations. It was well understood by the prophets that when "floods of ungodly men" overflowed the peoples, "then the earth shook and trembled; the foundations of heaven moved and shook, because He [God] was wroth" (2 Sam. 22:5, 8).

The sure word of prophecy assures us that as it has been, even so shall it be, until the heavens and the earth that now are, shall give place to the new heavens and the new earth wherein dwelleth righteousness. The apparent relation between the iniquities of men and the mighty convulsions of nature caused even Gibbon, the infidel deist, to confess, *"The natural order of events will sometimes afford strong appearance of moral retribution."* To understand what Gibbon meant, it is only necessary to recall that when, in 1902, old Mount Pélee buried its 40,000 inhabitants under a mass of burning lava, that city was acknowledged to be "the wickedest spot in the West Indies." The quake and the eruption were preceded by appalling degradation and unspeakable wickedness. Blasphemous rites, mockeries upon all things holy, were in progress. On Good Friday a pig was masqueraded through the city, and then crucified! Thereupon, it seems, nature arose in extreme wrath. One man alone, and he confined in a dungeon, lived to tell the tale!

A Modern Pompeii.

Mount Pélee was but a modern replica of old Pompeii. That beautiful city, the fashionable resort of wealthy Romans, while satisfying all the tastes and senses that art and luxury can satisfy for man, was at the same time bent on satisfying every foul instinct of human nature. Suddenly, "in the year A.D. 79 the volcano of Vesuvius began to groan and bellow with internal anguish, and then vomited forth columns of cinders and torrents of lava such as no preceding or succeeding age has equaled. . . . Pompeii perished in a shower of cinders and ashes. . . . The burial was complete" (Ridpath). Nature again had wreaked her vengeance on the violators of the laws of God.

Let *Blackwood's Magazine* (June, 1906) tell the story of the San Francisco quake, immediately after it happened:

"And when, on the morning of April 18th, 1906, earthquake and fire suddenly wiped out San Francisco, we are told by those well acquainted with the facts that in 'that gorgeous city of the West' . . . 'that California Sodom' . . . 'that refined sink of most positive iniquity' . . . not only had 'fair, dignified, and educated women' acquired the opium habit, but the aristocracy in general were given over to lust and vice. And thus having 'flaunted its unparalleled iniquities for nearly sixty years, Providence (at length) saw fit to intervene for the purification of that City of the Plain'!"

Let *The Evangelical Christian* record the story of the quake that totally destroyed the flourishing and extraordinarily beautiful city of Messina, Italy. In the early morning of December 28, 1908, the temblor struck, and 84,000 human beings died. We read:

"Only a few hours before that devastating earthquake, which laid Messina and the surrounding districts in ruins, the unspeakably wicked and irreligious condition of some of the inhabitants was expressed in a series of violent resolutions which were passed against all religious principles. While the journal *Il Telefono*, printed in Messina, actually published in its Christmas number an abominable parody daring the Almighty to make Himself known by sending an earthquake! And in three days the earthquake came!"

Our most recent quakes would also justify the belief that there exists an intimate relation between the moral and physical

worlds—that when the one suffers, the other suffers. Consider
the catastrophe that struck Tokyo only a few years ago, in
1923. Japan was admittedly the most immoral of civilized nations, and the Tokyo quake was the most terrible upheaval in
modern times.[1]

As I write, the wires are flashing, and the radio waves are
telling the story of an appalling disaster that has befallen Turkey, on the shores of the Black Sea. The earth there is still
shaking. Windrows of the dead are being piled high. The
latest report is that 46,000 are dead, with more dying. Their
cities completely demolished, tens of thousands are wandering
about without food, shelter, or warmth. Floods also have carried hundreds into eternity. It was reported that many persons had become deranged as a result of earthquake experi-
ences. The city of Erzincan suffered most, and a survivor
reaching Ankara (Angora), the capital of Turkey, said: "Erzincan is no longer a city, but a great necropolis. . . . Hundreds of bodies are still buried under the wreckage." A total
area of 4,000 square miles was stricken by the earthquake, and
terror-maddened cattle stampeded in western Turkey. "Most
water mains, railway tracks, and viaducts were shaken apart
like match sticks. Minarets and mosques also toppled."

Was Turkey Innocent?

We are hearing some complaints about "the goodness of
God." God's goodness needs no defense. However, it may
be well to remind the world at this moment that God is just,
even as He is good. The streets of the Turkish cities, now
piled high with debris commingled with corpses whose only
requiem is the groaning and the moaning of the dying—these
are the same streets whereon men, women, and little children
were slaughtered without mercy only a few short years ago.
Who can forget those Armenian massacres, when an expectant
Armenian mother was cut open with less pity than if she were

---

[1] NOTE.—While their connection with national sin is not so obvious,
two of the greatest earthquakes in history occurred in China in recent
years: one in 1920, in which almost 200,000 perished; another in 1927,
in which estimates of the slain greatly exceed 100,000.

a rat—when thousands of defenseless men, women, and little children were driven before daggers and guns into rivers to drown? Thus the Armenians were either massacred or driven out of that now unhappy territory. The rivers that then were clogged with the bodies of Armenians are *now* clogged with the bodies of Turks! Nature once more appears to be the avenger of a just and holy God!

From the divine revelation we have of the ways of God, one is compelled to believe that, apart from the merely natural reasons for our very recent earthquakes, and apart from the possible retributive aspect, there is another aspect that should concern us all. No devout believer in the inspired Word of God will ignore the fact that earthquakes, under certain circumstances, also are to be regarded as signs. When His disciples asked the great Master, "What shall be the sign of Thy coming?" (Matt. 24:3), He began His reply by saying: "Nation shall rise against nation . . . and there shall be famines, and pestilences, and *earthquakes* in divers places" (Matt. 24:7). When God sent John to the Isle of Patmos to bring before his astonished eyes a great panorama of the momentous events that shall draw man's day upon the earth to its close, that seer beheld earthquake after earthquake.

Great Earthquakes Still to Come.

He beheld, and saw God's last two witnesses to men, Elijah and Enoch (or, possibly, Elijah and Moses) slain on the streets of Jerusalem. "And the same hour was there *a great earthquake,* and the tenth part of the city fell, and in the earthquake were slain of men seven thousand" (Rev. 11:13).

He beheld, and when the sixth seal was about to break, "lo, there was *a great earthquake*; and the sun became black as sackcloth of hair . . . and every mountain and island were moved out of their places" (Rev. 6:12-14).

He beheld, and when the seven angels with "the seven trumpets prepared themselves to sound," there were "thunderings, and lightnings, *and an earthquake*" (Rev. 8:5).

He beheld, and when "the seventh angel sounded . . . there

were lightnings, and voices, and thunderings, *and an earthquake,* and great hail" (Rev. 11:15, 19).

He beheld, and when the angel of the seventh and last vial of God's wrath "poured out his vial into the air":

"There came forth a great voice out of the temple, from the throne, saying, It is done: and there were lightnings, and voices, and thunders; and there was *a great earthquake,* such as was not since there were men upon the earth, so great an earthquake, so mighty. And the great city was divided into three parts, and the cities of the nations fell" (Rev. 16:17-19).

What are we to understand as to the significance of all these earthquake phenomena? The Word of God alone can give answer. It was first given by the prophet Haggai, over five hundred years before Christ; and reaffirmed by the writer of Hebrews, nearly seventy years after the birth of Christ:

"For thus saith the Lord of hosts: Yet once, it is a little while, and I will shake the heavens, and the earth, and the sea, and the dry land; and I will shake all nations; and the desire of all nations shall come; and I will fill this house with glory, saith the Lord of hosts" (Hag. 2:6, 7).

The words of the prophets ring so clearly that they need no interpretation. All nature will convulse. All nations will shake. *Then* "the desire of all nations shall come." "The desire of all nations" is the "Wonderful, Counsellor, Mighty God, Everlasting Father, Prince of Peace" (Isa. 9:6). No matter what the ambitious, bloodthirsty dictators of earth may desire, the desire of the peoples of all nations is *peace.* Jesus Christ is that peace. When He shall come, "He shall speak peace unto the nations" (Zech. 9:10, R. V.). Therefore, we conclude that great convulsions of the earth's surface will immediately precede the return of our Lord from the heavens.

The writer of Hebrews gives further light. We read:

"Now He [God] hath promised, saying, Yet once more will I make to tremble not the earth only, but also the heaven. And this word, Yet once more, signifieth the removing of those things that are shaken, as of things that have been made, that those things which are not shaken, may remain. Wherefore, receiving a kingdom that cannot be shaken, let us have grace, whereby we may offer service well-pleasing to God with reverence and awe: for our God is a consuming fire" (Heb. 12:26-29, R. V.).

There, indeed, we have light. An earth shaking as it never has shaken in any like period of time before will be the God-given sign that the kingdoms of this world, which can be shaken, must give place to the Kingdom of God, which "shall stand for ever" (Dan. 2:44). Therefore, the seer on Patmos saw, and "there was a great earthquake. . . . And the kings of the earth . . . say to the mountains and to the rocks, Fall on us, and hide us" (Rev. 6:12-16). Why? Their kingdoms were to pass away! Likewise, when the seventh angel sounded, there was an earthquake, and "the nations were angry"! Why? Because the voices of Heaven were crying: *The kingdoms of this world are become the kingdoms of our Lord, and of His Christ"!* (Rev. 11:15). Hence, as the very last act before the white horse rides forth from the heavens (Rev. 19:11), "There was a great earthquake, such as was not since men were upon the earth, so mighty an earthquake, and so great" (Rev. 16: 18). Why? Because the cities of the nations were to fall (Rev. 16:19) and pass away for the coming of the "city which hath foundations, whose builder and maker is God" (Heb. 11:10).

In view of these many Scriptures, and since within the space of forty years we have now witnessed seven of the greatest quakes of all time (Mount Pélee, San Francisco, Messina, Tokyo, two in China, and Turkey), is it an idle fancy, born of desire, that causes us to believe that the nations of the earth now shaking must soon give way to the nation that cannot be shaken? "So likewise ye, when ye see these things come to pass, know ye that the kingdom of God is nigh at hand" (Luke 21:31).

(THUD! Right this instant, while I was penning those words, it felt as if some celestial giant with his great fist had tapped the church wherein I am writing! The building quivered. My secretary looked at me. I looked at her. We both

exclaimed, "Earthquake!" It was only a little California re-
minder, probably without special significance—but quite interesting *at this identical moment!* It becomes all the more
interesting when it reminds me that just two days ago my good
friend, Dr. Louis T. Talbot, pastor of the Church of the Open
Door in Los Angeles, was speaking over the radio. He was
referring to the Turkish earthquakes. He had just said that
he believed that they were very significant and were indicating
the closing hours of our age, and that he expected that they
would increase in number and in intensity. Those words were
scarcely off his lips when an earthquake struck and was the
hardest "bump" that Southern California has experienced since
the disastrous quake of March 10, 1933. Maybe this was
without any special significance, nevertheless quite interesting,
and I insert these two incidents here for the contemplation of
my readers.)

The late Sir Oliver Lodge, reputed to be the world's greatest
physicist, said only several years ago: *"I do not know the reason, but there is abundant proof that the earth's crust is at
present in an unstable condition."* The great physicist may
not have known the reason, but it may be that humble believers
in the words of God could have helped him a bit in his understanding on this subject.

On an upper bookshelf, just before me as I write, is a little
wooden cross, hewed out by the hand of some whittler and
presented to me by "The Others Class" of the First Brethren
Church of Washington, D.C. On the morning of March 10,
1933, this cross stood where it now is, with other mementos
and gifts from missionaries. At six o'clock on the evening of
that day, the Long Beach earthquake struck. While the earth
was still trembling, I climbed over the debris in the streets to
my study to see what damage here had been wrought. The
thousand volumes on these shelves were piled high on the floor.
The floor lamp was prostrate, and ink bottles, paste, and other
desk paraphernalia were likewise on the floor. I pushed away
books to find a stepping place and came in to view the chaos.
On the west side of the room the books in disorder were stacked

high. Those gifts and mementos were mixed all through the heap of books. Squarely on top of all that pile was a book by Dr. W. Lamb of Australia, with its title printed on a slant in large black letters across the front of the cover:

THE WORLD
in
CONVULSION

And, behold, that little wooden cross stood squarely on this cover, absolutely upright, and without a thing against which to lean! And, what made it seem all the more miraculous, that little wooden cross was top-heavy in its construction. The earth was still shaking, and had been shaking every few minutes since the main shock, but *there stood that cross!* What kept it there, absolutely upright on that book, with that title glaring at me? Well, the reader himself must judge. Could you blame me for standing there and singing?

> "In the cross of Christ I glory,
>   Tow'ring o'er the wrecks of time;
> All the light of sacred story,
>   Gathers round its head sublime.
>
> When the woes of life o'ertake me,
>   Hopes deceive, and fears annoy,
> Never shall the cross forsake me;
>   Lo! it glows with peace and joy."

One thing I know, that on this shaking old earth, "tow'ring o'er the wrecks of time" the cross still stands! And another thing I know: the kingdoms that can be shaken must soon pass away, that the Kingdom that cannot be shaken may come! For that Kingdom we wait! Come, come quickly, Lord Jesus, come!

XI

WHY THE END OF THE AGE MUST
BE VERY NEAR

I BELIEVE that the rapture of the Church must be very near, because I believe that *the Lord Jesus Christ will not break His word.* To do that would make Him a sinner like unto the first Adam; and this world, without a spotless Lamb, would have no Savior. I cannot help but wonder if supposedly Christian men know what they say when they speak their doubt as to the incarnate God keeping His covenants inviolate, and His promises immutable.

And remember, the incarnate God, Jesus Christ, could not have man's excuse for breaking a covenant or failing in a promise. Man, lacking foreknowledge, might enter into a covenant that he could be excused for breaking. A "covenant with death" *should* "be disannulled," and an "agreement with hell" should "not stand" (Isa. 28:18). But the all-wise God, seeing the end from the beginning, cannot have the slightest excuse for making a covenant He *cannot* keep; or for making a promise to which He *will not* be true. In the light of His absolute foreknowledge, to break a solemn promise would be to lie. To lie would be sin. The Savior would need a savior! That cannot be. God will keep His covenants! Jesus Christ will keep His promises!

Christ Will Keep His Promise.

Now then, let us *suppose* that the writer, with divine foresight given him, should peer into the future, and fully know the things that are to be. And then suppose that he, about to go away on a long winter journey, should solemnly promise his wife: "Retta Virginia, when the fig tree in our garden puts forth its buds, and the mocking-bird is feeding its young in a nest in its branches—*watch! In that day* I'll come back to you!" Then suppose "that day" comes. The tiny fig buds push through the bark, and the mocking-bird, having made her nest early, now feeds her young high up among the branches. Then my beloved gets herself ready, watches out of her window— *waits!* She murmurs: "The fig tree blossoms. The mocking-bird feeds her nestlings. He said he would come. Surely he will!" And surely he *will*, unless he is false to his word!

Once upon a time the Lord Jesus sat on the side of Olivet, where He so loved to be. He talked to His disciples about going away to receive a crown, and then to return. Their hearts were heavy at the thought of the separation. They had come to love Him dearly. They had left their nets—their all—to follow Him. He had become their all in all! Without Him, what would they do? Knowing the agony within their hearts, He solemnly promised them, *"If I go . . . I will come again"* (John 14:3). Could they be blamed for having asked Him, "Tell us . . . what shall be the sign of Thy coming?" (Matt. 24:3). Certainly not! And surely, if He answered that question, He did not deceive them with His answer.

And answer that question He did! He even went into the details, when He told them of "things" that would "come to pass." He said plainly, "When ye shall see *all these things,* know that it [My coming] is near, even at the doors" (Matt. 24:33). Again: *"Then* shall they see the Son of man coming in a cloud with power and great glory . . . when these things *begin* to come to pass, *then* look up, and lift up your heads" (Luke 21:27, 28).

Some ill-advised souls are fond of quoting His words, "But of that day and hour knoweth no man, no, not the angels of heaven, but My Father only" (Matt. 24:36), with the intent to have us believe that we are not to concern ourselves with the time element in connection with our Lord's return. But they seem not to know—or, are not honest enough to confess that they know—that in the same breath the Master said: "When ye shall see all these things, KNOW *that it is near"* (Matt. 24:33). We are *not* to "know" the exact day and hour of His coming. Hence the folly of setting exact dates. We are to "know" by sure signs when He will be "near, even at the doors." Hence the folly of blinding oneself to impending events of tremendous importance—the most momentous events that possibly can come to the world of men—the resurrection of the righteous dead, the changing of the mortal bodies of the living saints to immortal bodies, the translation of the righteous to meet the Lord in the air, the coming of the Antichrist, the return of Christ with His saints, the overthrow of Satan and all his hosts, the restoration of the throne of David, the judgment of the nations, the millennial reign of Christ, and the peace and glory that shall never pass away. There is only one reason why any man may not be interested in the nearness of events like those. That reason is—*he lacks any firm belief in those things!*

Peter's Warning.

Some years ago the writer was conducting an evangelistic campaign in a church in a city in the midwest. I announced that I was going to preach one night on "The Signs of Our Lord's Return." The pastor came to me and said:

"Bauman, I wish you would omit speaking upon that particular subject. Preach, if you wish, that Christ is coming back to earth again some day, but let 'signs' alone."

I said: "Why should I let 'signs' alone?"

"Because," he said, "there aren't any 'signs.' Show me one!"

I replied: "There is one just three feet in front of me!"

Then, instantly throwing open my Bible, I turned to 2 Peter 3:3, 4, and read: "Knowing this first, that there shall come in the last days scoffers, walking after their own lusts, and saying, Where is the promise [Gr. *epaggelia,* that is, *promise, announcement, proclamation, assurance—the sign or thing that proclaims and assures*] of His coming?" And then I said: "And here you stand, my brother, a scoffer, scoffing *at what?* Scoffing at every sign that is proclaiming and assuring the early return of Jesus Christ back to this world that needs Him so! Brother, you have asked me for a sign. Behold *yourself!*" He turned on his heel and said: "Aw, you disgust me!" I replied, as he walked away: "Well, brother, the disgust is mutual!"

When signs stand out, as they do today, like mountain peaks —when God in His goodness is trying to warn a sinful world by every possible token that judgment impends—for men deliberately to close their eyes and their ears, and sneer at the warnings that the incarnate God Himself gives them—can only fill one with disgust, if pity could leave room for disgust.

The Lord Jesus said, "When ye . . . *see* . . . *these things*." Then He evidently expected reasonable men to "*see* these things." Again, when He said, "Know ye that the kingdom of God is nigh at hand" (Luke 21:31), He evidently expected reasonable men to "*know*" when the kingdom is nigh.

Yes, "there shall come in the last days scoffers . . . saying, Where is the promise of His coming? for since the fathers fell asleep, all things continue as they were from the beginning of the creation" (2 Peter 3:3, 4). And isn't just *that*—even as Peter declared nearly twenty centuries ago it would be—the disparagement of the unbeliever? How often have those of us who believe to be *bona fide* the signs our Lord gave—how often have we been told: "These signs always have been! War, famine, pestilence, earthquake, false prophets, apostasy, anti-Semitism—the apostles talked of these things even in their day; our fathers in the tenth century saw these signs in their day and looked for the Christ to come; saints back in 1844 saw these 'signs,' sold their goods, put on white robes, and went forth to meet Him!" So speaks the scoffer today. But these twentieth-century scoffers were not unseen by the prophets of old.

Yet there are some things of which the twentieth century scoffer is woefully ignorant. "For of this they willingly are ignorant" (2 Peter 3:5), that the signs our Lord gave His disciples were never seen before in their fullness as they are being seen today; and *many of them were never before seen at all!* When the Kingdom of God is at hand, when the appointed time for our Lord's return to earth is here, then not one, nor two, nor three of the signs given must appear; but *all* the signs must appear—not one can fail. And they must "stand out" in such a way that the saints can *know*.

Now, with all due respect to all those who did "put on their white robes" in days long past, I wish to affirm, without hesitation or equivocation, that *at no time* since our Lord uttered

His great prophecies have any goodly number of the signs been present *contemporaneously*,—that is, at the same time. And contemporaneous they must be!

XII

SIGNS OF THE END THAT HAVE NEVER OCCURRED BEFORE

PERHAPS some of our fathers, in their eagerness for the return of their Lord from Heaven with all the blessings He shall bring, saw signs where there were none. But far better that we should err as they did than to sit without desire, indifferent as to whether our heavenly Bridegroom shall come tonight or a thousand years hence. When He shall appear, God grant us this—that He shall know that we, with bridal heart, yearned for His presence!

Especially is this true in view of our Lord's earnest request and solemn warning: "Watch ye therefore . . . lest coming suddenly He find you sleeping. And what I say unto you I say unto all, Watch" (Mark 13:35-37). Will He have to say to us in that day as He said to the Pharisees and Sadducees at His first advent: "When it is evening, ye say, It will be fair weather: for the sky is red. And in the morning, It will be foul weather to-day: for the sky is red and lowering. O ye hypocrites, ye can discern the face of the sky; but can ye not discern the signs of the times?" (Matt. 16:2, 3).

Now in answer to the scoffer's sneer that there is no visible sign of our Lord's return to earth, inasmuch as "all things continue as they were from the beginning of the creation" (2 Peter 3:4), I shall proceed to point out at least fifteen divinely given signs of our Lord's return that are now *here,* and that never were here before the dawn of our twentieth century. Most of them may be regarded as coming within the last twenty-five years! Some of these signs have been pointed out in previous chapters; but in listing the fifteen in this chapter I must now refer once more, though briefly, to those also.

I. The Synchronization of the Greatest War, Greatest Famine, Greatest Pestilence, and Greatest Earthquake of All Time.

As we have before observed, as our Lord sat on old Olivet His disciples asked Him a very plain question: "Tell us . . . What shall be the sign of Thy coming, and of the end of the world [consummation of the age]?" (Matt. 24:3). Christ's reply was equally plain: World war, famines, pestilences, and earthquakes in divers places (*Cf.* Matt. 24:7).

The Greatest War.

The war from 1914 to 1918 was a war such as this earth has never before known. Its battle lines were literally flung around the earth. It was the first *World War.* From the most authentic statistics available, gathered by the New York *Evening Post,* the New York *Tribune,* and from other sources, in England as well as America, we learn that more than 58,500,000 men were in arms! Of that number, more than 10,000,000 names were recorded on the death roll on the field and in the army hospitals. Deaths as a direct and indirect result of that war reached the appalling figure of 37,000,000! Crammond, the well-known English statistician, sets the direct cost of that war at $210,000,000,000; and the direct and indirect cost at $370,-000,000,000. The debts of the nations at the close of the war were ten times what they were before, and that staggering burden has been increasing ever since. That war made all others that this bloody old earth has ever known seem pygmy. Viscount Grey sized up the matter about right, we believe, several years ago when he said: "I think it is certain that if there be another such war, civilization will never recover from it!"

And now, what are the prospects? Only a score of years have passed; and, while the whole earth is still writhing from the wounds of that war, the imbecilic, cutthroat highbinders who have slugged and gunned their way to seats of dictatorial power have launched another world catastrophe that bids fair to make the World War of 1914-1918 look like a small child's affair! Only one whose sanity is open to question can blind himself to the significance of the present world situation in the light of Christ's words in Matthew 24.

The Greatest Famines.

On the heels of this holocaust came the first great Chinese famine. The London *Times* (Dec. 15, 1920) gave a summary of it. "The population now totally destitute in Chihli is 6,000,000; in Shantung, 2,500,000; in Honan, 3,500,000; in Shensi, 1,000,000; in Shansi, 500,000—a total of 13,500,000." How many starved to death will never be known.

Then, only eighteen months later, the Volga valley in Russia, actually the most fertile land in Europe, was swept by famine in 1921, and wilted as under the breath of hell. No Joseph was there to save. The Archbishop of Canterbury said at the time: "Never in the history of the world has a condition of things existed comparable to the ghastly death by famine of whole millions of men, women, and children." The famous Doctor Nansen, having accurate knowledge, said: "The famine is beyond all doubt the most appalling that has ever happened in the recorded history of man." The greatest famine theretofore was the Chinese, in the middle of the nineteenth century, when five thousand perished daily. "Thirty thousand Russians," wrote D. M. Panton of London, "are dying of starvation every day." The cemeteries had to be guarded to keep them from being rifled for cannibalism. The horror of it all beggared description.

Then came a third and yet greater famine disaster. "As nearly as can be estimated," said the *Federal Council Bulletin* editorially in May, 1929, "over 20,000,000 women and children in China are now not merely facing starvation, but actually starving. Many of these are in regions too far inland and away from rail communications to be helped now." The Chicago *Tribune* declared that "latest reports on the famine indicate 30 million persons are affected instead of the 20 million first reported. . . . Competent authorities expressed fear that 15,000,-000 persons might perish." In North China alone, the China

Famine Relief, U.S.A., with headquarters in New York, printed in its appeal: "The tragedy of over 8,000,000 human beings having starved to death is one of the most terrible in history"; and then (Mar. 30, 1931) feared the death of 2,000,000 more "before another crop is harvested." Certain it is that this famine was the worst in all the records of man. Dogs, cats, and rats were delicacies. The cooking and eating of the flesh of dead relatives was common. Thousands died with tree bark, roots, and grasses stuffed in their stomachs. White clay was made into soup to deaden the agonies of hunger. This meant only slow suicide and more agonizing death later on.

The Greatest Pestilence.

Without any warning, except that which fell from the lips of Christ Himself nearly two millenniums before, a pestilence came in 1918, the total mortality of which was not less than 12,000,000, placed by many at a much higher figure. The medical correspondent of the London *Times*, as early as December 18, 1918, reported: "Six million persons have perished of influenza and pneumonia during the last twelve weeks. . . . This plague is five times more deadly than war. Never since the Black Death has such a plague swept over the face of the world."

But the Black Death was the scourge of *Europe* and was more or less localized. The Black Death was *epidemic*. The "flu" of 1918-1919 was *pandemic*. No country on earth escaped its ravages. It broke out on ships two thousand miles from land. In some countries, true, it was more deadly than in others. In India, 4,933,133 deaths were recorded within a few months. Whole villages became villages of the dead. "It is an epidemic," declared Major Norman White, Sanitary Commissioner for India, "in many respects without parallel in the history of disease."

The Greatest Earthquakes.

We have before and elsewhere noted that the greatest earthquakes (save for possibly one) that have ever shaken this old *terra firma* have all come since the close of the World War.

Several of them literally shook the whole terrestrial globe. An official report of the Chinese quake in December, 1920, gave the loss of life around the Ching Ting Choo district at 300,000. A C.I.M. missionary declared that "working on this proportion, it would mean that somewhere between 500,000 and 1,000,000 lost their lives." Whether or not these figures are accurate, certain it is that this quake exceeds any other earthquake known in seismographical records. Only one earthquake earlier in human history might contest the "honor" of being the greatest, and that would be the Indian earthquake, in 1737, when an estimated 300,000 died. As good an authority as the *Encyclopœdia Britannica* says that this figure "may be exaggerated."

Since that time Japan, Baffin Bay, India, and Turkey have experienced major quakes, while the crust of the whole earth has been aquiver with lesser quaking.

Easier to Sneer Than to Think.

Greatest war, greatest famine, greatest pestilence, greatest earthquake—any one of which should cause men to meditate upon the way of God with men. And when all these can be synchronized within the space of ten years—1914 to 1923—and a space of twenty years would include the *last* great Chinese famine, then men who *think*, and especially those who *think* in the light of divine revelation, will not dismiss it all with a flippant sneer. I said—*men who think!* Most men don't *think*. It is so much easier to sneer!

Weigh it well! Nearly six thousand years have passed since God placed Adam in Eden. And yet the four greatest plagues that can afflict the human race were all packed recently *in a single decade!* If that does not fulfill the sign that the Lord Jesus gave in answer to the question "What shall be the sign of Thy coming?"—then, pray tell, just what is it going to take to fulfill the words that "cannot be broken"? (John 10:35).

But now note: *"All these are* [but] *the beginning of sorrows"* (Matt. 24:8). One would think that those four sore calamities were sorrows enough! But our Lord warns us that they will be only a prelude to the "sorrows" that are to be!

Then, "O my Lord, what shall be the end of these things?" (Dan. 12:8).

And now, behold, what have we seen come upon the world since those four stupendous cataclysms upheaved man's cosmos to the point where the entire structure is severely threatened with collapse and utter destruction?

II. Anti-Semitism Engulfs the Jewish Race.

Bear in mind, our Lord was speaking to Jews, not Gentiles. So far as the Jews are concerned, their latest period of "sorrows" did not begin with the World War, famine, pestilence, and earthquake in the years between 1914 and 1923. Their world agony began with the advent of the violently anti-Semitic Reichsfuehrer, Adolf Hitler, who stepped into full power in Germany, March 5, 1933. From that day, wave after wave of anti-Semitic hatred, starting in Germany, has rolled out over the nations of the whole earth. It is admitted that at no period since the prophecy was uttered by our Lord have so great "sorrows" engulfed the "brethren" of Jesus as the "sorrows" they have known since the German Jewbaiter began to breathe forth his sulphuric hatred of all Israel. "Then!" When? *"Then"—immediately after* the greatest of all wars, famines, pestilences and earthquakes—*"Then* shall they deliver you up to be afflicted, and shall kill you: and ye shall be hated of all nations for My name's sake" (Matt. 24:9).

Can any man, cognizant of the facts of the present-day events as those events touch the sons and daughters of Israel, fail to realize that our Lord's prophetic utterance is being fulfilled to the last jot and tittle? The virus of Jew-hate has been and continues to be injected into the arteries of the nations until the whole earth sickens and staggers as if bereft of all reason. On and on it plunges into such a day of slaughter and horrible agonies that thinking men are saying it will bring back the midnight of a barbarism more barbaric because of our modern instruments of torture and of death—an age darker than the darkest midnight this earth has ever known.

And what started the march to the international slaughterhouse? Let the man who started it, and knew he was starting it when he marched his armies into Poland, give answer. He should know. He recently declared that the Jew is back of it all—"the *international* Jew"—"the *capitalistic* Jew"—that he says is ruling Britain and France and New York.

"But," someone asks, "is it not only a recurrence of that which has been so often before?" Do not "all things continue as they were from the beginning of the creation"? Not so! Heretofore, when the Jew was persecuted in one nation, some other nation offered him a haven. Today, he is literally a vagabond upon all the seas of the earth. No welcoming hand waves to him from any harbor.

Davar, a labor paper in Palestine, recently vividly described the sorrow of the Jew out on the waters that bathe the shores of the homeland that God gave to him: "From the Greek isles and Mediterranean ports the cry of Jewish refugees languishing in distress is heard day by day. In the ports of Lebanon are shiploads of refugees suffering from hunger and disease, people beyond all hope, wandering purposelessly without prospect of rest. The authorities in the Lebanon, and the French officials, fulfill their duty by fumigating the boats stricken with plague, *and then dispatch the refugees back to sea.* . . . We hear of nine hundred refugees brought to a distant island and deposited without anyone caring for their fate."

It never has been thus before! And especially is it true that no outburst of anti-Semitism in the history of man has been *immediately preceded* by synchronized war, famine, pestilence, and earthquake such as previous ages have not known!

The international blockade is against the race that introduced us to the living God, gave us our Saviour, and of whom the Master said, "Salvation is of the Jews" (John 4:22). The spirit of anti-God is abroad on the face of the whole earth. Therefore, the Jew is hated, as our Lord Himself declared, "for My name's sake!" Yes, the *international blockade of the ports of earth against the brethren of Jesus* is significant beyond our power to tell! Heretofore they were permitted to wander on the land. Now they must wander on the sea, with no land they can call their own. Verily, *"There is sorrow on the sea; it cannot be quiet"!* (Jer. 49:23). No, "it cannot be quiet"

with the Jew a wandering, homeless vagabond upon its bosom!
It never, never will be quiet until Israel is permitted to *land!*
Until then—

> "To and fro,—to and fro,—
> Sorrow and weeping,—
> Strange seas to roam.
> To and fro,— to and fro,—
> Yet ages are ending! for
> Israel is riding the
> Mad billows home!"

III. Scoffers Deriding the Promise of the Lord's Return Are Evidencing Among Professed Christians a Strange Hatred of "The Blessed Hope"—a Hatred Heretofore Unknown in the History of the Church.

As we have before indicated, scoffers would have us believe
that the "signs" to which students versed in the Word of God
are pointing today, as revealing the nearness of our Lord's return, are but conditions and events that have appeared from
time to time throughout past ages, and therefore that as "signs"
they have failed. But did our Lord make a grave mistake and
in ignorance assert that there would be revealing signs in the
time of the end? He said: "AND THERE SHALL BE SIGNS
. . . *and then shall they see the Son of man coming in a cloud
with power and great glory. And when these things begin to
come to pass, then look up, and lift up your heads; . . . know
ye that the kingdom of God is nigh at hand*" (Luke 21:25-31).

Are we to scoff at these words, and thus impugn either the
wisdom or the truthfulness of the Lord Jesus Christ? Are we
to believe that He would tell His disciples in the clearest possible language that, when certain well-defined events take place
upon the earth, they are to "look up" in glorious expectancy;
and then, when those events actually take place, that He will
not return, thus leaving His own people in bitter disappoint-
ment and subject to the world's ridicule? God forbid!

When the heavens shall open, and the Christ, on His great
white charger, shall ride forth, there shall be written across
His brow in letters of vivid flame, for all doubters of "the sure

word of prophecy" to read: "FAITHFUL AND TRUE"!
(Rev. 19:11.) Not one word that His prophets have spoken
shall fail!

Doubters as to the literal return of the Lord there have been
among professed Christians through the centuries. But it is
left for this "advanced" twentieth century to produce the crop
of sarcastic sophisticates to whom Peter refers. Even if one
blinded by "the wisdom of this world" should be persuaded
that the idea of a personal and visible return of Christ from the
heavens is fanciful and untrue, what sort of spirit within him
is it that urges him to speak *derisively* of such a hope—a hope
that has sustained and comforted the hearts of countless millions who have had to wade through "seas of blood" in their
pilgrimage home to the Father's house? One would think that
any true-hearted child of God, if unable to believe in the personal and visible return, would recognize at least the fact that,
to those who believe it, it is precious and sustaining. He would
appreciate that back of such a belief can exist only a loyalty,
devotion, and love for the Christ that died for us, beautiful to
behold.

But no! Professing to be Christian, and ofttimes sitting
among the ordained ministers of the Church, these scoffers delight in mocking at the "blessed hope" that has buoyed so many
discouraged souls and kept them betimes from utterly sinking
in despair. Especially comforting and sustaining is this hope in
this present hour of the deepest distress this world has known
in all its troubled history. In fact, it is the *only* ray of hope
piercing the blackness of the hour! Sometimes these scoffers
are even bishops who penalize those under their dominion for
believing—*what?* Simply that the One, "Whom having not
seen" they love, is coming back some day for His own!

Such a hope many of these church leaders consider a foolish
idea in the minds of misguided souls—misguided because they
believe that their Lord and Savior meant exactly what He
said! It matters not to these scoffers that there is a tremendous
array of testimony to show that the hope of the personal and
visible return of our Lord was a "blessed hope" within the
breasts of the choicest of the saints throughout the centuries.

No less distinguished a personage and devout Christian than Sir Isaac Newton, nearly three hundred years ago, grasped the full meaning of Peter's prophecy as he wrote:

"About the time of the End, a body of men will be raised up who will turn their attention to the prophecies, and insist upon their literal interpretation in the midst of much clamor and opposition."

Assuredly that "body of men" has been "raised up"; and "much clamor and opposition" is right! Derisive scoffers, standing amid signs that tower like mountain peaks all about them, shut their eyes to them all and yawn: "Where is the promise of His coming? All things continue as they were!" *Such a condition has not been before!*

IV. Peter's Prophecy and the Bible Calendar Indicate That Man's Six Days for Labor Upon the Earth Are Swiftly Drawing to a Close. The Gentile Sunset Is at Hand.

A Divine Hint to the Saints.

In the day when the scoffers' sneer shall be heard throughout Christendom the true saints of God are provided with a wisdom that this world knows not. When the world's intelligentsia begin their torrents of ridicule against "the sure word of prophecy," Peter protests: *"The Lord is not slack concerning His promise, as some men count slackness"* (2 Pet. 3:9). Then he addresses himself to the saints to give them wisdom from above: *"But, beloved, be not ignorant of this one thing, that one day is with the Lord as a thousand years, and a thousand years as one day"* (2 Pet. 3:8).

It is as much as to say: "Children of God, when 'that blessed hope' within your hearts becomes the object of derision on the part of an apostate apostleship, and they ask, 'Where is the promise of His coming?' I give you a hint: *'one day is with the Lord as a thousand years, and a thousand years as one day.'* Keep that 'one thing' in mind, and you shall know."

It is plain that Peter intended to give special knowledge to tried and perplexed saints. But wherein, in that "one thing" that he sets forth by inspiration of the Holy Ghost, is there light and knowledge? To say, as some do, that "a thousand years" means "a long, indefinite period of time" is to make the statement mean absolutely nothing. It must mean that a thousand years is a thousand years—nothing more, nothing less.

The Seventh Day a Sign.

Now the day of our Lord—that day when the saints of God "shall be priests of God and of Christ, and shall reign with Him a thousand years" (Rev. 20:6)—is to be Israel's day of rest, a day which they heretofore "entered not in because of unbelief" (Heb. 4:6). To the children of Israel, Jehovah, through Moses, declared that the seventh-day Sabbath was to be a "perpetual covenant": *"It is a sign between Me and the children of Israel for ever:* for in six days the Lord made heaven and earth, and on the seventh day He rested" (Exod. 31:17). All of which means that the seventh-day Sabbath is a purely Jewish institution, a sure "sign" and a "perpetual covenant" *between Jehovah and the sons of Jacob.* Count "a thousand years as one day," says Peter. The seventh day is Israel's rest day. It is the day of which the Lord God of Israel says:

"In that day I will raise up the tabernacle of David that is fallen . . . and I will build it as in the days of old . . . And I will bring again the captivity of My people of Israel, and they shall build the waste cities, and inhabit them; . . . and I will plant them upon their land, and they shall no more be pulled up out of their land which I have given them, saith the Lord thy God" (Amos 9:11-15). "And in that day there shall be a root of Jesse, which shall stand for an ensign of the people; to it shall the Gentiles seek: and *His rest shall be glorious"* (Isa. 11:10).

Now if Israel's rest day is the *seventh* day, and is a day of one thousand years, then the six days that must precede the seventh day logically must be days of equal duration—*therefore, six thousand years.* To man it was said: "Six days may work be done; but in the seventh is the sabbath of rest" (Exod. 31:15). "Six days shalt thou labour, and do all thy work"

(Exod. 20:9). Six thousand years man has been given on this earth to accomplish his work. The seventh is the Lord's rest—the millennium.

This view that the seventh thousand years of human history will be the world's day of rest is a view that has been commonly accepted by many of the world's greatest Christian scholars.

Bishop John Newton, commenting on the twentieth chapter of Revelation, said:

"That the Jewish Church before John, and the Christian Church after him, have believed and taught that these one thousand years will be the seventh Millenary of the world. A pompous heap of quotations might be produced to this purpose, both from Jewish and Christian writers" (*Dis. on Proph.*, pg. 587).

Then, likewise, Bishop Latimer affirmed:

"The world was ordained to endure, as all learned men affirm . . . six thousand years. . . . Therefore, all those excellent and learned men, whom, without doubt, God hath sent into the world in these latter days to give the world warming, do gather out of Scripture that the last day cannot be far off" (*Sermon on The Lord's Prayer, No. 3*).

We quote also that great Church father, Lactantius (260?—325?):

"The sixth thousand year is not yet completed, and when this number is completed, the consummation must take place, and the condition of human affairs be remodeled for the better" (*Div. Insti.*, B. 7, ch. 14).

"The irradiation of Elias" (Elijah) was commonly accepted among the Jews:

"The world endures six thousand years, two thousand before the law, two thousand under the law, and two thousand under the Messiah."

So common was this tradition among the Jews, that they used it constantly in their arguments in apostolic times.

The Sun Now Setting on the Eve of the Sixth Day.

It is an interesting fact that the world's four greatest Bible chronologers—Clinton, Bowen, Jarvis, and Usher—are, at farthest points, only about one hundred years apart in their estimate as to the number of years since Adam was placed in the Garden of Eden "to dress it and to keep it" (Gen. 2:15).

Clinton states that the period of time from Adam's creation to the First Advent of Christ was a period of 4138 years. Bowen gives the figure, 4128 years. Jarvis holds to the figure 4019 years; while Usher, whose chronology is usually found in our Bibles, gives 4003 years. When we strike an average of the four estimates, we find that, *according to the figures of the four chronologers,* 6012 years have passed since Adam began man's work on the earth!

We are setting no exact dates, simply because we have no exact dates to set. Nevertheless, it appears that the best calendar that man possesses indicates that the sun is setting upon the sixth thousand-year-day of man. And, *as the sun is setting, behold what momentous and tremendous events we see transpiring in all the earth!* Verily, *this hour has not been before!*

Thanks be to the apostle Peter, through whom God gave us this wisdom! We are commanded to "be not ignorant of this one thing." Therefore, we refuse to be ignorant: THE SEVENTH DAY IS AT HAND! "The Lord is not slack concerning His promise, as some men [the scoffers] count slackness" (2 Pet. 3:9). The night is far spent. The daybreak is at hand. Therefore, ye saints of God: "Rest in the Lord, and wait patiently for Him: fret not thyself because of him who prospereth in his way, because of the man who bringeth wicked devices to pass. . . . For yet a little while, and the wicked shall not be: yea, thou shalt diligently consider his place, and it shall not be. . . . The Lord shall laugh at him: for He seeth that his day is coming. . . . But the meek shall inherit the earth; and shall delight themselves in the abundance of peace" (Psa. 37).

Paradoxical as it may seem, the day of the "abundance of peace" is to be immediately preceded by a day in which a man

—a rider upon a red horse—shall "take peace from the earth" and men shall "kill one another" (Rev. 6:4). *Has that rider gone forth?* Some believe he is even now riding.

V. The World-Wide Preparation for War on a Scale Never Before Conceived by the Mind of Man.

I doubt that there is a passage in all the Bible more significant of the hour in which we live, more timely for the meditation of the saints of God, than the third chapter of the prophet Joel.

Armageddon is the day of which Jehovah says: "I will . . . gather all nations, and will bring them down into the valley of Jehoshaphat, and will plead with them for My people and for My heritage Israel, whom they have scattered among the nations" (Joel 3:2). It is the day when the Lion of the Tribe of Judah "shall roar out of Zion, and utter His voice from Jerusalem . . . the hope of His people, and the strength of the children of Israel . . . [and] then shall Jerusalem be holy, and there shall no strangers pass through her any more" (Joel 3:16, 17). And that day is to be immediately preceded by a world-wide preparation for battle such as man has never witnessed in all the ages past. Hear the voice of the prophet, speaking more than twenty-seven centuries ago: *"Proclaim ye this among the Gentiles; Prepare war, wake up the mighty men, let all the men of war draw near. . . . Beat your plowshares into swords, and your pruninghooks into spears: let the weak say, I am strong. Assemble yourselves, and come, all ye Gentiles"* (Joel 3:9-11).

However, the voice of another prophet, Isaiah, spoke of a glorious day in which the nations *"shall beat their swords into plowshares, and their spears into pruninghooks: [when] nation shall not lift up sword against nation, neither shall they learn war any more"* (Isa. 2:4). Idealists have been fond of quoting this last Scripture, looking forward unto that day. But the idealists have usually failed to note the fact that that long desired day is to be immediately preceded by a day when the nations shall do the very opposite—beat their plowshares into swords and their pruninghooks into spears! The Gentile powers shall literally exhaust their resources in order to create more and more of the instruments of war and destruction, and shall consume the instruments of peace for this purpose.

Discouraged souls, who have been listening to the gurgle of blood in Czechoslovakia, Poland, Finland, Norway, Holland, Belgium, France, England, China, and elsewhere during the past few weeks, in their increasing pessimism are beginning to believe that the idea of a warless world is an idle dream. Let them be of good cheer! "The darkest hour is just before dawn." And that proverb stands, so far as the coming of the warless Golden Age is concerned. The morning after the day when the blood of men shall flow "even unto the horse bridles" (Rev. 14:20) will be the dawn of the new day wherein the Prince of Peace shall mount His throne in David's royal city and "nations shall learn war no more."

Can any thoughtful soul read Joel's words and fail to see that in this, *our* day, they are meeting with positive fulfillment? *"Prepare war"!* For this very purpose, for many months, practically every nation on earth has been engaged in an under-the-carpet hunt for a few more nickels and dimes with which to pay for the building of more battleships, more destroyers, more battle planes, more bombers, more submarines, more guns, more gas masks—more of everything pertaining to war. This world of men, in all its gory story, has never seen anything even to compare with this fateful hour. Our own supposedly peaceful nation is appropriating billions and ever more billions to "prepare war"! Without stopping to consider the staggering burden of debt that is to fall upon the shoulders of our children, we plunge on—no matter what the cost—in preparation for the day of Armageddon! Billions upon billions throughout all the nations, until the brain reels trying to comprehend the staggering sums. Even as I write, the Congress of these United States is appropriating billions and ever more billions to put a navy in the Atlantic, and another in the Pacific—a two-ocean navy that can whip the world! And, now, Russia announces that she will build a larger one! And so the race goes on! Unless there is no such thing as a sign and its fulfillment, then we have a sign and its fulfillment here. And, *it has not been so before!*

Naturally, the "prepare war" sign leads on to another sign closely related.

VI. Violence in All the Earth Such as Could Not Have Been Known Even in the Days of Noah.

Speaking of His return to establish the Kingdom of Heaven, our Lord said: *"And as it was in the days of Noe, so shall it be also in the days of the Son of man"* (Luke 17:26). And violence was one of the outstanding features of "the days of Noe." It is written: *"And God said unto Noah, The end of all flesh is come before Me; for the earth is filled with violence through them; and, behold, I will destroy them with the earth"* (Gen. 6:13). Violence—a universal reign of anarchy—brought on the judgment of the flood.

But what shall we say of this Year of Our Lord 1940? It isn't *war* that we are seeing today. War is too dignified a word to express it. It is violence! It is anarchy! It is cold-blooded murder! War recognizes certain laws. In the past, even in the hell of war, certain laws have been recognized by the nations. Soldiers were courageous enough to wear their own uniforms. Non-combatants—especially women and little children—were supposed to have some rights and human consideration. Red Cross hospitals were not intentionally violated. Now and then some foamy-jawed brute afflicted with the rabies wandered about, but he was an exception rather than the rule. Today, certain nations no longer stop even to declare war, much less to trouble themselves about its laws. They simply sneak out in the dark and start butchering everything in sight. Perhaps they do not declare war because they know it isn't war they expect to wage!

The men who ride the saddles in Germany, Italy, Russia, and Japan today are international assassins, hatchet men that would make our once dreaded Apache Indians grow green with envy. Nero may have fiddled while Rome burned. But women and little children in Rome had a chance to flee the flames. These modern cutthroats, running amuck in Europe, Asia, and Africa, dance in fiendish glee while mothers with babes on their breasts, and with not the slightest chance to flee, are blown to bits. Countless thousands of little children sob and moan, and groan and choke, and gasp and die in horrible agonies.

When von Hindenberg was still President of the German Reich, the Nazi leaders were training German youth to hate, and to exult in cruelty. Nazi youths sang their battle song as they paraded the streets of Berlin:

> "When hand grenades burst all around,
> Our heart's contentment knows no bound."

And thus was reared the generation of ravaging beasts that so recently exultingly informed the world that they hadn't even made a good start yet in their work of enslaving and torturing men and women and little children, and despoiling the earth.

But here is a source of real comfort—here is the silver lining in the terrifying cloud. When once *violence* again fills the earth, the God of Israel, even our God, according to His promise "will shake all nations, and the desire of all nations [even the Prince of Peace] shall come: and I will fill this house [even the house of Israel] with glory, . . . [and] the glory of this latter house shall be greater than of the former, saith the Lord of hosts: and in this place will I give peace" (Hag. 2:7-9). Yes, in that day, "He shall save the children of the needy, and shall break in pieces the oppressor. . . . He shall have dominion . . . from sea to sea, . . . and His enemies shall lick the dust. . . . In His days shall the righteous flourish; and abundance of peace so long as the moon endureth. . . . All nations shall call Him blessed" (Psa. 72). "They shall not hurt nor destroy in all My holy mountain . . . and His rest shall be glorious" (Isa. 11:9, 10).

> "Our Father which art in heaven,
> Hallowed be Thy name.
> *Thy kingdom come!*"

VII. Israel Revives, and the Fig Tree Puts Forth Its Leaves for the First Time Since Nebuchadnezzar Lopped Off Its Branches.

It was early in August, 1914. Delegates out of practically all the nations were wending their way to Vienna for an international peace conference. War was to be banished from the earth and mankind was on the march to universal brotherhood —according to these idealists. Suddenly, without warning, old Mars released his dogs, and those who had come to make peace forsook their mission and scurried for home.

Then, one morning, my telephone rang. The trembling voice of a mother asked: "Dr. Bauman, what do you think of this terrible war? Does the Bible have anything to say about it?" My answer was: "It is just another war, such as have come and gone for centuries, *unless* this conflict should bring to pass two possible events:

"*First.* Should Turkey enter this war, and be driven out of Palestine; and then, should Palestine be restored to the Jews for a homeland, the most significant event possible will have taken place.

"*Second.* Should Italy enter this war, and a new Cæsar be born in Rome, with the revival of the Roman Empire as his program, then the next most significant event possible will have taken place."

At that time neither Turkey nor Italy had gone into the war. Both of them later went into the conflict, and the two events of which I spoke came to pass. To this day I have had no reason to alter my opinion then expressed.

The "Prophet-of-God" Captures Jerusalem!

It was in 1917. Out of Egypt marched a long line of British Tommies. At the head of that line marched the British General Allenby. "Allah-Bey! Prophet-of-God!" cried the Turkish soldiers in Jerusalem; "when a leader by that name comes, Jerusalem must go back to the Jews!" For such had been a tradition of the Moslem priesthood for centuries. The Turks decided not to waste their ammunition! Without firing a shot they took to their heels, headed for Constantinople! General Allenby, man of the magic name, walked peacefully into the city, and more than thirteen centuries of Moslem rule, and exactly four hundred years of Turkish rule, came to a sudden end. Previously, Lord Balfour had issued his famous Declaration, promising that Palestine, when once delivered from the rule of the Turk, should become the homeland of the Jews. Apparently the centuries-old dream of Israel was about to be fulfilled.

Palestine's Revival.

At once a vast system of Jewish mass migration was planned, with offices in London and Copenhagen. And though Britain, later, under Arab pressure, cooled in the matter of completely fulfilling her promise to the Jews, yet tens of thousands of Jews wended their way back to Zion, and today there are 425,000 Jews in Palestine, whereas as late as 1867 there were not more than 10,000.

"The Palestine Restoration Fund" was organized. From all over the world millions upon millions of dollars poured in. The Jews "bought" with "money" every foot of land that the Arabs would offer for sale. It is written: "Behold, I will gather them out of all countries . . . and I will bring them again unto this place . . . and fields shall be bought in this land. . . . Men shall buy fields for money" (Jer. 32:37, 43, 44).

Thousands of acres of swamp land were reclaimed. The modern harbor at Haifa was built. New villages sprang up everywhere. The great modern and purely Jewish city of Tel Aviv, now well beyond 100,000 population, came into being. Railroads, highways, and canals were constructed. Water supplies were conserved. Desert wastes, dead for centuries, sprang to life. Today, blossoming like a rose, Palestine vies in its glory with Southern California. The great Jewish University on the eastern slope of Mount Scopus was erected, and General Allenby was present at the laying of its cornerstone. Instead of the Yiddish, the ancient Hebrew was prattled by the little children on the streets. It was written: "Then will I turn to the people a pure language" (Zeph. 3:9). With Jehovah there is only one earthly language that is pure—the Hebrew. Verily, the fig tree is budding! *It has not done so before!*

In that long ago, as the Jew of Jews sat on the brow of old Olivet, His "disciples came unto Him privately, saying, Tell us, . . . what shall be the sign of Thy coming, and of the end of the age?" (Matt. 24:3). "And Jesus answered and said . . . Now learn a parable of the fig tree; When his branch is yet tender, and putteth forth leaves, ye know that summer is nigh: so likewise ye, when ye shall see all these things, know that it is near, even at the doors" (Matt. 24:32, 33).

One is prompted to ask: Did the Lord Jesus mean what He said? If He did, then He is not only coming back to earth again, but He is "at the doors." And if the fig tree is budding, not all the bitter enmity of the Arabs, not all the patrolling gunboats of the nations, not all the driving power of the godless Hitler-Mussolini-Stalin combine, can keep the sons and daughters of Israel from landing back upon their sacred shores. Omnipotence has spoken it: *"The house of Jacob shall possess their possessions"* (Obad. 17).

Be it known that the restoration of the Jewish nation is not dependent on any human arm. It depends solely upon the arm of the Lord God of hosts: "Thus saith the Lord God, Behold, O My people, I will open your graves, and cause you to come up out of your graves, and bring you into the land of Israel . . . *I the Lord have spoken it, and performed it"* (Ezek. 37:12, 14).

The world, even Christians, in this present hour thinks upon the Poles, the Finns, the Norwegians, the Dutch, the Belgians, the French—all victims of a powerful nation run amuck. Men are forgetting the real victim of Hitlerian madness—the one who has suffered longest and most cruelly. The man who was first to fall among thieves—the man who was first to be stripped, wounded, and left to die—the man almost forgotten and who is doomed to suffer most in the present world turmoil —is the man on whom the eye of the omnipotent God is fixed. The Jew is still "the apple of His eye" (Zech. 2:8). Let us not be led astray. If you want to walk in the light, *watch the Jew!*

VIII. The Roman Empire Revives for the First Time Since the Northern Invader Laid Its Ancient Glory in the Dust.

"The scripture cannot be broken" (John 10:35). It is written: "And the ten horns *out of this kingdom* [Rome] are ten kings that shall arise" (Dan. 7:24). "And in the days of these kings shall the God of heaven set up a kingdom" (Dan. 2:44).

The Roman Empire Must Live Again.

The "ten toes" of the great image beheld by Nebuchadnezzar in his dream belonged to that part of the image that was *Rome*. The "ten horns" on the fourth beast beheld by Daniel in his dream belonged to that beast that was *Rome*. The "toes" and the "horns" are one and the same. They both prefigure Rome in its last formation—the Roman Empire as it will appear when "the Stone of Israel" (Gen. 49:24) shall fall from the opened heavens and grind to dust all Gentile dominion, power, and glory. *The Roman Empire* MUST *be here for the falling of the Stone* (Dan. 2:34, 35, 44, 45). And it is evident that that Empire will appear in its final form as a ten-kingdomed confederacy. Not only Nebuchadnezzar and Daniel saw it in their dreams, but the Seer of Patmos toward the close of his awe-inspiring vision beheld the monster:

"The ten horns which thou sawest are ten kings, which . . . [shall] receive power as kings one hour with the beast. These have one mind, and shall give their power and strength unto the beast. . . . For God hath put in their hearts to fulfil His will, and to agree, and give their kingdom unto the beast, until the words of God shall be fulfilled" (Rev. 17:12, 13, 17).

Federation—A Vain Hope.

It is of interest to note that many of the minds that guide the ships of state have been and now are looking toward just such a concourse of nations for the salvation of our "civilization."

Years ago, shortly before his death, the great British statesman Lord Salisbury said: *"Federation is the only hope of the world."*

Several years ago Prof. Julian Huxley, British biologist, speaking before the American Association for the Advancement of Science, compared the smaller States of Europe to little animals, and the mighty totalitarian nations of Germany, Russia, and Italy to "giant reptiles of the Mesozoic age, carnivorous, heavily armored animals like the tyrannosaurs, stegosaurs, and ceratopsians." Present events prove that his comparison was apt. He then declared that the world's hope lay in the formation of some kind of world-state in which everyone would be a world citizen.

Edouard Daladier, formerly Premier of France, on December 29, 1939, asserted that France and Great Britain were "inseparably united even beyond victory," and suggested that other governments support a plan for the creation of a European federation of States after Hitlerism is crushed.

But vain is the hope of man that some concourse of nations will bring forth his Utopia. Isaiah, predicting the Assyrian invasion of Israel, looked far beyond that invasion when he wrote:

"Associate yourselves, O ye people, and ye shall be broken in pieces; and give ear, all ye of far countries: gird yourselves, and ye shall be broken in pieces. . . . Take counsel together, and it shall come to nought. . . . For the Lord spake thus to me . . . and instructed me . . . saying, Say ye not, A confederacy, to all them to whom this people shall say, A confederacy; neither fear ye their fear, nor be afraid. Sanctify the Lord of hosts Himself. . . . And He shall be for a sanctuary" (Isa. 8:9-14).

And then, turning his eyes away from all the sanctuaries of men as places of refuge from the storm, the old prophet turned his eyes toward the heavens and cried: *"I will wait upon the Lord, that hideth His face from the house of Jacob, and I WILL LOOK FOR HIM"* (Isa. 8:17). Good advice, indeed, for Israel twenty-seven centuries ago! Good advice for Jew and Gentile today!

"The Resurrection of the Empire."

When the Italian dictator came into power nearly a score of years ago, he wrote his Fascist creed. The last article read: *"I believe in the genius of Mussolini, and* IN THE RESUR-RECTION OF THE EMPIRE."

Many months ago, with Libya already in his possession, this resuscitator of the Empire marched his legions down into Ethiopia and annexed that ancient kingdom to his own. His only excuse was: "The Empire must be revived, glorious as it was in the days of Augustus Cæsar."

With Ethiopia in his clutches, the dictator proclaimed the return of the Empire, and Italy now bears the official title—*"The Roman Empire."* She has dated her official documents thus: *"R.R.E. 1927"*; i. e., *"Revived Roman Empire, Year 5"*—five years after that October day when Mussolini marched into Rome and compelled the Italian king to "sign on the dotted line." And, whether the world appreciates the fact or not, *the Roman Empire is a reality*—very, very much upon the map of the world today. Since the proclamation of the existence once again of the Roman Empire as a political entity, the mighty Fascist fist calmly reached across the Adriatic and drew Albania to the Empire's motherly bosom! And now she is reaching out her mailed fist, backed ostensibly by the German sword, after Syria, Iraq, Palestine and Egypt! How significant!

No such revival of Rome has this world seen before!

Let us not, in this hour of turmoil and stress, be misled by the immediate successes of the German octopus from Berlin. As I write these words, Hitler's mechanized Juggernaut has rolled over Paris, and is now storming the gates to Britannia, expecting to turn London into an ash heap. The German Attila looks like a world conqueror! Hitler may revel in his present victories. Any success of his will be exceedingly temporary. God's revelation will not fail because of the tanks and planes of this new cock of the walk! The *prophetic* seer will keep his eye fixed, not upon the banks of the Rhine, but upon the banks of the Tiber!

The Shrewd Strategy of Mussolini.

In Rome reigns a dictator who may be likened unto a man whose life was endangered by two giant enemies on the highway. The man did not have strength to cope with either of them, but, with most cunning and subtle stratagem, he succeeded in beguiling and maneuvering them into mortal combat. Having done that, he sat off to one side, hoping there would be some remains worth sacking. At a strategic moment he stepped into the fray. It remains to be seen whether he can gather the much desired booty into his Mediterranean boot.

No shrewd mind can conceive that Mussolini has any affection for Adolf Hitler. No man who has watched the shrewd dictator in Rome play his game can believe that Mussolini will be fool enough to help *permanently* an ancient enemy and an uncertain present "friend" to set himself up in mighty power just across an imaginary line. That far-sighted Roman, the political world's most crafty strategist, must gloat within himself as he shakes his mailed paws high in the air and does his war dance on the side lines, while the German gourmand gluttonizes himself into a state of exhaustion. He even professes friendship for him and seemingly helps him gluttonize. Doubtlessly, he is perfectly willing and very happy to have his German "axis" partner crush to earth both France and England. But "in his heart of hearts," he is hoping that Germany will bleed nigh unto death in the operation! The Roman bides his time!

When, one of these days, the Italian dictator cools toward the "Rome-Berlin Axis" (and stranger things have happened), we need not be surprised to see a weary, choking, and all but exhausted German vulture fall at the feet of an old grizzled Bear (Russia) for protection. Then behold the final power and glory of "The King of the North," so well known to the students of the unfailing Word of prophecy. Talk about war planes! The King of the North boasts that he has 20,000 of them, and many more thousands building! Talk about man power! The King of the North points to 17,000,000 men ready for arms! Talk about resources! The King of the North has immense reservoirs yet untapped. That Bolshevist monster "out of the north parts" (Ezek. 38:15) is the real nightmare of the world! Mussolini sees the specter in his dreams by night and in his visions by day. And, despite all denials to the contrary, the sniffle and the grunt at the back door to Adolf Hitler's tent is causing that scalping Apache some mental pains also!

Now, as I have pointed out several times before, "ten kings," whose dominions are within the boundary lines of the ancient Roman Empire, suddenly are going to *"have one mind, and shall give their power and strength unto the beast"* (Rev. 17:13). Kings do not give over their power to anyone without some compelling reason for doing so. The great Northern Confederacy will furnish a most compelling reason.

Mussolini has long been working on his Mediterranean bloc. That is a matter of common knowledge. Adolf Hitler *may* be the rider on the "red horse" and "take peace from the earth" (Rev. 6:4). He *seems* to be fulfilling that rôle. But he is *not* the rider on the "white horse" that is to go forth "conquering, and to conquer" (Rev. 6:2). Adolf Hitler will never succeed in destroying England. Adolf Hitler is not *the* Antichrist! When the Antichrist comes, the Jews will hail him as their Messiah. Our Lord said to the Jews: "I am come in My Father's name, and ye receive Me not: if another shall come in his own name [Dan. 11:36; 2 Thess. 2:3, 4], *him ye will receive"* (John 5:43). Can anyone, by the wildest flight of imagination, conceive of the Jews receiving Adolf Hitler as their Messiah?

The world is witnessing in this hour two gigantic powers in Europe, Russia and Italy, who are watching while the rest of the nations bleed themselves white. They are shedding little of their own blood. In due time, each of these powers will gather to itself its own proper allies. Then these two powers— Bolshevist and Fascist, both godless but hating each other with a hellish hatred—will complete their final mobilization, the one "in the north parts," and the other down in Egypt. God's clock will strike the hour. Then, in all the fury of the damned, they will rush at each other's throats. The one will rush "out of the north parts" (Ezek. 38:15; 39:2). The other up from his rallying point in Egypt (Dan. 11:42-44). They will meet on the plain of Jezreel, the valley of Esdraelon, along the southeastern slope of Mount Carmel. There, on ground already the most blood-soaked soil of earth, will the Russian-Germanic hordes be cut to pieces by the federated Roman power. Gog will be given a place of burial in the valley henceforth to be known as "The valley of Hamon-gog" (Ezek. 39:11).

Flushed with victory, the Roman, supreme dictator of ten kingdoms, head of the armies of *all* the nations (Rev. 13:7), parading under his own flag of flags, will follow the steps of all his predecessors and deify himself. Then he will set up an image of himself for men to worship (Rev. 13:8, 14-18). The last of all the Cæsars will then have only one more march to make—to Armageddon! But that must be left for another chapter!

Military chieftains now believe that he who can rule the skies can conquer the earth. *Up there,* far above all principality and power, God reigns! We rest in the blessed assurance that soon He will reign *down here!*

IX. The World Was Recently Stunned to See the German Black Eagle Wrap Its Mighty Talons Around the Great Paw of the Russian Bear in Friendly Union—a Spectacle Men Never Witnessed Before.

Perhaps nothing in the astonishing events of modern times was more astonishing than the alliance recently consummated between Adolf Hitler and Joseph Stalin. To understand the marvel of it all, one has only to refer to a statement in Hitler's now famous volume, *Mein Kampf:*

"It must . . . never be forgotten that the present rulers of Russia are low, bloodstained criminals . . . the scum of humanity . . . and have exercised the most gruesome tyranny of all time."

Was Hitler lying when he wrote that description of his present "friend," Joseph Stalin? *I think not!* He was telling the exact truth. But, with no apologies whatever for those words and others like them, how did it become possible for these two men to grasp each other's hand in friendship? There is only one explanation—they are "birds of a feather." None other than they, who are "bloodstained criminals . . . the scum of humanity" themselves, would ever stoop to ally themselves with "bloodstained criminals . . . the scum of humanity!"

A deluded world has believed that these two "beasts" were sworn enemies, supposedly bitter-enders for political philosophies diametrically opposed to each other. It seemed utterly impossible that they ever could wrap their arms around each other's necks save for the purpose of strangling each other to death. But when God's Word is at stake, and "the scriptures must be fulfilled," impossible things immediately become possible.

The unfailing Word of God reveals that the two mighty empires of Russia and Germany will be firm allies when the stage is once set for the final acts of our age. They will march and fight together until the bones of their vast hordes shall lie to bleach for "seven months" "upon the mountains of Israel" (Ezek. 39:4, 12). "Gomer [Germany], and all his bands" (Ezek. 38:6), will be allied with "Gog" (Russia) in the time of the end, and together they will "think an evil thought" that will cause them to prowl down into Emmanuel's land—

"to take a spoil, and to . . . prey . . . upon the people that are gathered out of the nations. . . . And thou shalt come up against My people Israel. . . . It shall be in the latter days. . . . And it shall come to pass at the same time when Gog shall come against the land of Israel, saith the Lord God, that My fury shall come up in My face. . . . And I will call for a sword against him throughout all My mountains, saith the Lord God: . . . And it shall come to pass in that day, that I will give unto Gog a place there of graves in Israel, the valley of the passengers on the east of the sea: and it shall stop the noses of the passen-

gers: and there shall they bury Gog and all his multitude"
(Ezek. 38 and 39).

What an inglorious end for Adolf Hitler and Joseph Stalin
and all their allied hosts—the stench of them literally shall
cause passengers passing through the land to hold their noses.
And for "seven months shall the house of Israel be burying
. . . them, that they may cleanse the land" (Ezek. 39:12).
The mighty Hitler, who fully expects soon to have the joy of
burying Israel,—he, if yet alive, and if not alive, then his
"pure Aryan" hosts—at last *will be buried by Israel!* No
wonder Adolf Hitler hates the Old Testament and its Jew!
No wonder Joseph Stalin is the world's most implacable foe of
all that is called God!

How perfectly the characters of these two dictators that now
terrorize the whole world fit into the prophetic picture of
Ezekiel! Both are anti-God (38:3); both delight in polluting
the name of Israel and of Israel's God (39:7); both have
their ravenous eyes upon "the land of Israel" (38:18); both
are spoilers of weak and defenseless nations (38:11); both
are enemies of, and indifferent to, the protests of "Tarshish
[Britain], with all the young lions [Canada, United States,
Australia, New Zealand, South Africa] thereof" (38:13); each
heads "a mighty army" (38:15); both in military tactics
"ascend and come like a storm" (38:9); and both are so
morally rotten that even now the world's passengers hold
their noses as they pass by! (39:11).

Verily, the union of these two Frankensteins is a matter of
prophecy—*a sign that has not been seen before!*

X. All Nations Today Are in Distress Hitherto Unprecedented, Perplexity Heretofore Unknown, Animosities Erstwhile Unparalleled, and Fear Aforetime Unsurpassed.

No living man today, in the same number of words, could
describe the actual physical and mental state of the world more
accurately than did our Lord nearly twenty centuries ago:

"And there shall be . . . upon the earth distress of nations, with perplexity; the sea and the waves roaring; men's hearts failing them for fear, and for looking after those things which are coming on the earth" (Luke 21:25, 26).

Weigh well these words of the Master:

"There shall be . . . distress of nations." The pages of history have no record of *international* distress such as confronts all nations in this present hour. Demonized men never before have possessed such powerful instruments of torment, devastation, and death, as they now possess, which are enabling them in a few short months to waste the wealth that it has taken them centuries to accumulate, and to obliterate the civilization that mankind has been millenniums in building. Think of Hitler and Stalin, two depraved, sadistic maniacs, in whose twisted souls there is found no place for love, or justice, or mercy, or morality, or truth, whose only god is the god of force—two absolute despots whose underlings in governing are chosen from the most debauched classes, bitter anti-Semites, haters of the Bible, mockers at Christ, despisers of God, whose chief glory is their capacity to hate and to kill. The philosophy of both of them is expressed by Hitler in his book, *Mein Kampf:*

"Love is negative, while hate is positive. To win the masses, you must give them something to hate."

Therefore, the world is now seeing what an army, made up largely of youths around twenty years of age who from their childhood have been taught this philosophy of hate, and commanded by a ruthless tyrant who knows no pity, is capable of doing. Almost defenseless nations, innocent of any crime that gives cause for war, have been overrun and their people enslaved. Ask the Poles what it means. Ejected from their homes that Germans may occupy them, and driven into slavery! They are forced to slave in German fields. Again we see the philosophy of Hitler put into practice. "No civilization can exist without a foundation of slavery. New forms of slavery *must* be evolved." Well, Mr. Hitler, that idea is not new. Fifty-seven centuries ago, another slaver, named Pharaoh, believed the same thing!

Little wonder that all the nations of the earth not already fettered and daggered by these two Apaches are looking for bomb-proof shelters, donning hideous gas masks, and hiding underground in terror. Add to all this the staggering burden of debt that bears down on all nations, the fast mounting taxes, the lengthening bread lines, the vast unemployment, and on top of it all the necessity of increasing all their burdens by the hugest preparations for war that human history has ever known. This is "distress of nations" that *has not been before*— has not even been approached. If this is not a fulfillment of the Master's own prophecy, then just what does it take to fulfill a prophecy?

"With perplexity." The literal Greek rendering is: *"With no way out."* And what man lives who knows a "way out"? Who is even suggesting a "way out"? Men used to talk of a "social gospel" as a "way out," since it was to make good neighbors of all the nations of the earth. The "social gospel" program was backed by the world's intelligentsia, supported by millions of dollars in money, heralded to the ends of the earth, and believed in by vast masses of humanity. It had its chance. It signally failed. Men used to boast of "scientific advancement," and the new god, Science, was enthroned to be the savior of the world. It was supposed to "possess the stuff, to build a Paradise in time." Mankind has now rudely awakened from that dream. Mankind is shrinking in terror before the working of ninety per cent of the stuff that Science has put into the hands of the children of men.

What a marvelous achievement it was when the Wright Brothers of Dayton, Ohio, first sent their heavier-than-air ships afloat into the ethereal blue! Millions of men, women, and little children now look up into the ethereal blue with faces paled by terror. The fact of the matter is, mankind would be infinitely better off if no airplane had ever sailed into the air. The story is told of a well-to-do old German who had a sick wife. Every time the doctor came, the old German was told that his wife had "improved." One day the wife died. Later, some one asked the old German what caused the death of his wife. "Ach," he said, "mine vife died mit improvements!" Exactly so! The human race seems about to commit suicide by the use of its own "improvements"! The "horse and buggy days" were not altogether bad! Men now know something of the meaning of Solomon's words: *"Lo, this only have I found, that God hath made man upright; but they have sought out many inventions"* (Eccles. 7:29).

Back in 1914-1918 men still believed they had some "way out." A "League of Nations"—a "World Court"—a "World Made Safe for Democracy"—a "War to End War"—these were some of the panaceas freely offered. All have "gone with the wind." There is no talk of *any* remedy now. All rulers, all political councils now talk of nothing else than how to build more speedy airplanes, more deadly gases, more destructive bombs, more invulnerable tanks, more armies of hate—but the veriest fool knows that that is no "way out." *That* is the pathway to hell on earth! No wonder the great Master, looking down through the centuries and beholding our day, cried: "Except those days should be shortened, there should no flesh be saved" (Matt. 24:22). No wonder the prophet Isaiah, also beholding our day, wrote: "The earth . . . shall disclose her blood, and shall no more cover her slain" (Isa. 26:21). No "way out"! Never before have men been so conscious of the fact!

"Men's hearts failing them for fear, and for looking after those things which are coming on the earth." Need we comment upon these words? Need we say more? Any close student of history will be quick to tell you that never before has there been an hour like unto this,—never before a day when the whole concourse of the nations was filled with such terrifying fears of the morrow,—a day when "all faces shall gather blackness" (Joel 2:6). Hermann Rauschning, former Nazi President of the Danzig Senate, says: "I know Hitler's intentions . . . his world-revolutionary alliance with Soviet Russia, the projected destruction of France, the breaking up of the British Empire,

his designs upon the American hemisphere and his march into colonial areas,"—in short, the subjugation of the civilized world.

There are said to be more than eight hundred organizations in America right now which in one form or another are the stooges of the rampant dictators. (America, you *need* to have a fear!) "I do not believe," shouts the German war lord, "that there can be peace among the nations until they have the same law and the same system of law. [He must mean the law of the jungle!] That is why I hope that National Socialism [Nazism] will one day extend over the whole world. This is no fantastic dream, but an achievable object. . . . Almighty God, bless our weapons, bless our combat!"

Just what "Almighty God" Hitler is asking to bless his weapons does not appear. Certainly it is not the "Almighty God" of the Jew! But these words of Adolf Hitler clearly reveal the dream of the totalitarian dictators before whom all the world feels so helpless in this awful hour! No wonder that every Jew, every Christian, every idealist, every lover of peace, every lover of justice, every lover of liberty have "hearts failing them for fear."

But let the heart of no true believer be found among the hearts that are failing for fear, "for looking after those things which are coming on the earth." This world's outlook is not ours. Remember, if the great prophecy uttered by our Lord nearly two thousand years ago is being thus fulfilled to its last jot and tittle, insofar as it should be fulfilled up to date, it is certainly not for us to believe that that *part* of the prophecy yet to be fulfilled shall fail.

Remember the promise of our Lord: *"And when these things begin to come to pass, then look up, and lift up your heads; for your redemption draweth nigh"* (Luke 21:28). Some may say that these words were spoken to the children of Israel, and not to Gentile believers. If true, that matters not; for our hope is bound up with "the redemption of Israel."

Yea, the Lover of us all solemnly promised: *"Then"*—when these conditions prevail upon the earth—"shall they see the Son of man coming in a cloud with power and great glory" (Luke

21:27). He said He would come—*then*! The very honor of our Lord is assuredly bound up in the keeping of that promise. "He is faithful that promised!"

Therefore, be still, my heart! Let no haunting fear disturb thy peace, even though "nations at their base are crumbling"! The eye of faith beholds, and the rainbow is about the throne! Hallelujah!

XI. The Great Apostasy That Has Overrun the Nations Within Christendom.

That an apostasy, in depth and extent never before realized, was intended by the Spirit of God, divine author of all Scripture, to stand as an infallible sign of the approach of the translation of the saints, is written as plainly as human language can make it:

> "Now we beseech you, brethren, by the coming of our Lord Jesus Christ, and by our gathering together unto Him, . . . the day of Christ . . . shall not come, except there come a falling away [apostasy; Gr., *apostasia*] first" (2 Thess. 2:1-3).

The word which the inspired writer used means "a falling away" from the theological beliefs *once held*. And not since the apostle penned those words has the world seen anything in the way of apostasy comparable to the apostasy that has overtaken the so-called Christian world.

Russia Is Apostate.

It is true that in Russia, Christianity for centuries had been a formal, lifeless sort of institution. Nevertheless a belief in the Bible, in the God it reveals, in the risen Christ it presented as a Savior, was maintained. Only in this last sad hour has it remained for a Lenin and a Stalin to profane everything holy in any religion that upholds the existence of a God to Whom men shall some day render an account. It remained for the puppets of the Russian government that now is, to tear the robes from the body of the priest and carry him away to a prison hell for daring to give the Holy Sacrament to a dying man! The sufferings which countless men and women and little children have had to endure in Russia because they refused to deny their faith in a living God are too foul for words and too terrible for description.

It may be pointed out that ancient Rome was equally a persecutor. But Rome clung to her gods—expressions of her belief in the supernatural. Russia knows no God and no gods— believes in *nothing!* Again, *Rome was never apostate,* for to be apostate you first have to be professedly Christian. Russia is utterly apostate—having fallen away from the faith she once espoused.

Germany Is Apostate.

Again, consider Germany. Who would have believed that the land that fostered the Reformation and gave us Luther would so quickly, if ever, foster the utter paganism of Nazism and give us Hitler? And this Austrian Frankenstein, who allies with himself in government the basest of base men—a monster that all the world knows to be an assassin—a red-handed murderer to whom the sweetest of music is the moans and groans of dying men and women, whose only crime is that they were born of Jewish blood—this is the man that Germany today would deify! Saints of the living God languish in his prisons; they have been forcibly closeted in pigsties at night; they have been barbarously beaten and subjected to unmentionable tortures. Yet no nation ever was blessed with greater spiritual light and opportunity. *Germany is apostate!*

In lesser degree, nation after nation has become apostate,— has turned away from the living God and has trampled upon His holy laws. We Americans are feeling a deep sorrow for France, compelled to capitulate before the godless German destroyer of nations. Our sorrow is natural, for France has been a sister republic, wherein men have been free. Yet France deliberately turned her back on God, and for more than one hundred and fifty years has been a hotbed for atheism. Thirty years ago her Premier, Maristide Briand, boasted: "We have driven Jesus Christ out of the army, the navy, the schools, the hospitals, the lunatic asylums, and the orphanages. We must now drive Him out of the State altogether" (*The Friend,* Sept. 17th, 1909). The man who guided France through the World War of 1914-1918, Clemenceau, was a bleak atheist. Nations that bow Christ out of their councils are nations that ever come to judgment. Such is the testimony of history.

America Becoming Apostate.

Our own America was born of men and women who deeply reverenced the Bible and the Christ it revealed. The textbooks in our public schools were filled with quotations from the Scriptures and with genuinely spiritual readings. Schoolmasters began the day with the reading of the Scriptures and with prayer. Today it is an offense against government in some of our states even to read the Bible, without comment, in our public schools. God, His Christ, and His Bible, have been politely bowed out of public schoolrooms at the behest of Jews, Roman Catholics, Communists, and infidels. Yet we wonder why the Lord God of Israel permits a debased warlord to make our hearts flutter with fear as we feverishly arm, and wonder what the morrow will bring forth.

Within the last few hours, as I write, I have listened to two governors and one senator from our great American commonwealths speak to the entire nation over the radio. All three of them spoke of our national peril. All three of them favored the rearmament program of the President of our nation. But all three of them also plainly stated that our woes have come upon us—to use the words of Oklahoma's governor—"because *we have forgotten God!*" He used strong language in his condemnation of the modernistic university professors who have led the youth of our nation away from God and the Bible. And he said plainly that they who are guilty are "not all university professors"! He was kind to a lot of ordained "pinks" in not naming them!

Ten years ago, George Herbert Betts (Methodist), Professor of Religious Education in Northwestern University, sent out questionnaires to 1,500 Protestant ministers, chosen at random from twenty denominations. Replies from 700 were received.

He tabulated the answers in a volume, *The Beliefs of 700 Ministers,* which was issued by the Abingdon Press (Methodist) of Cincinnati, New York, and Chicago. The result was startling!

Of the "700 ministers," 500 were settled as active pastors, 200 were still students in different theological seminaries. Several questions and the answers here will suffice.

"Do you believe that God is omnipotent?" *Of the settled pastors,* 87 per cent said "yes"; 4 per cent were "uncertain"; 9 per cent said "no." *Of the student preachers-to-be,* 64 per cent said "yes"; 7 per cent were "uncertain"; 29 per cent said "no."

"Do you believe that the creation of the world occurred in the manner and time recorded in Genesis?" *Of the pastors,* 47 per cent said "yes"; 5 per cent said "uncertain"; and 48 per cent said "no." *Of the students,* 5 per cent said "yes"; 6 per cent said "uncertain"; and 89 per cent said "no."

"Do you believe that the Devil exists as an actual being?" *Of the pastors,* 60 per cent said "yes"; 7 per cent said "uncertain"; and 33 per cent said "no." *Of the students,* 9 per cent said "yes"; 9 per cent were "uncertain"; and 82 per cent said "no."

"Do you believe that Jesus was born of a virgin without a human father?" *Of the pastors,* 71 per cent said "yes"; 10 per cent said "uncertain"; and 19 per cent said "no." *Of the students,* 25 per cent said "yes"; 24 per cent were "uncertain"; 51 per cent said "no."

"Do you believe that Jesus' death on the cross was the one act which made possible the remission of sins?" *Of the pastors,* 70 per cent said "yes"; 6 per cent were "uncertain"; 24 per cent said "no." *But of the students,* 29 per cent said "yes"; 10 per cent were "uncertain"; while 61 per cent said "no."

"Do you believe that after Jesus was dead and buried, He actually rose from the dead, leaving the tomb empty?" *Of the pastors,* 84 per cent said "yes"; 4 per cent said "uncertain"; 12 per cent said "no." *But of the students,* only 42 per cent said "yes"; 27 per cent were "uncertain"; while 31 per cent said "no."

"Do you believe that the New Testament is, and always will remain, the final revelation of the will of God to men?" *Of the pastors* only 66 per cent said "yes"; 10 per cent were "uncertain"; while 24 per cent said "no." *But of the students,* only 18 per cent said "yes"; 13 per cent were "uncertain"; while 69 per cent said "no."

In these figures, note the swift growing unbelief—the change in the figures from pastors to students. Note what the modernistic seminaries ten years ago were doing to the coming ministry in the Church of God. And during these past ten years these students have been operating! This is "apostasy"! No wonder that the men at the helm of our ship of state, seeing the dark shadows of an atheistic, liberty-destroying dictator falling over the earth, preaching his "gospel" of hate to the youth of the world with awful results, are crying out to the American people for a return to God!

As it is in America, so it is in Britain. The impetus of the forces of hell has become so strong, the representatives of the Devil are so deeply entrenched, that only help through a personally returning Lord can save us. And that means that the predicted judgments of God must fall—yea, already are beginning to fall—upon the nations.

One thing is evident, a great "falling away" is here, and *no such apostasy has ever been before.* Even in the "dark ages," while there were bitterness and hate and martyrdom, yet there was no such denial of God and the great fundamental doctrines as we see today.

But there is a bow in the cloud! It is when just such an apostasy has overtaken "Christendom" that "our gathering together [in the air] unto Him" (1 Thess. 4:13-18; 2 Thess. 2:1) is to take place, while on the earth "that man of sin [shall] be revealed, . . . who opposeth and exalteth himself above all that is called God" (2 Thess. 2:3, 4).

If those nations which have been flooded with the light from Heaven would repent and turn to God even now, and cry out for mercy, God would "hear from Heaven, and . . . forgive their sin, and . . . heal their land."

But will they do it? Then what true saint will deny God the right to bring to the nations His judgments? It will be better so! Our times are in His hands. We leave them there! And —*our Heavenly Father makes no mistakes!*

XII. The Preaching of the Gospel of the Kingdom for a Witness to All Nations.

This is a sign that has not been before!

"And as He [Christ] sat upon the mount of Olives, the disciples came unto Him privately, saying, Tell us . . . what shall be the sign of Thy coming, and of the end of the world?" (Matt. 24:3).

That was a fair question. It received a fair reply. That reply, in part, we now quote:

"This gospel of the kingdom shall be preached in the whole world for a testimony unto all the nations; and then shall the end come" (Matt. 24:14, R. V.).

There is only one conclusion to which we can honestly come, and that is this: When once "this gospel of the kingdom is preached in the whole world for a testimony," *our Lord must come!* He *said* He would. His veracity is at stake. And when the incarnate God's veracity is at stake, just one thing can happen—HE WILL KEEP HIS WORD!

Nineteenth Century Missionary Progress.

At the dawn of the nineteenth century, the Christian Church had little or no access to the heathen world. It is not necessary to discuss here the barriers that were erected between the Church and the unevangelized world that defied the wit, wisdom, and power of the Christian cohorts to surmount. But, not by might, nor by power, but by the Spirit of God, courageous men and women began to scale the walls of China, to unlock the sealed ports of Japan, to explore the "impenetrable depths" of Africa's forests, to defy the hostile English power that stood between them and the multitudes of the unevangelized in India, to challenge the hate, or indifference, of the Moslem world, and, to dare to be made food for cannibals upon the isles of the seas.

The result was that, except for some Moravian missionaries, missionary agencies carrying the Scriptures to the heathen world practically did not exist at the beginning of the nineteenth century; but, at the beginning of the twentieth century, the messengers of the Cross were either knocking at the gates of every nation on earth, or, had broken through those gates. By the year 1925, the statistics of the evangelical missionary societies of the world showed a *foreign staff* of 29,188 missionaries treading the highways of the nations proclaiming the riches of God's grace, and the coming of His kingdom to earth. Moreover, a *native staff of* 151,735 converted heathen were enrolled on records of the foreign missionary societies of the evangelical world, and they, also, were proclaiming the Gospel of the grace of God and of His coming kingdom to all men everywhere.

Also, at the beginning of the nineteenth century there were no Bible societies printing the Word of God to be read by the unevangelized millions of the children of men. Today, we have seen three great Anglo-Saxon Bible societies pouring forth annually over 14,000,000 portions of the Scripture in about 1,000 languages and dialects.

As a matter of fact, the nineteenth century witnessed the most amazing advancement that the Christian Church has ever known. And, when this Second World War began, it began in a world that was fully opened to the heralds of the Gospel, and the Gospel was being preached in all nations for a "testimony" to God's loving kindness toward all men.

The Gospel of the Kingdom, vs. the Gospel of Grace.

Moreover, let it be carefully noted that it was to be the "gospel of the kingdom . . . [that would] be preached in the whole world for a testimony." The "gospel [good news] of the kingdom" has not to do with the testimony as to the grace of God that was manifested through the atoning work of Christ, but it has to do with the *"return"* of Christ to "build again the tabernacle of David, which is fallen . . . [and to] set it up" (Acts 15:16). It has to do with the promise of God, made through Gabriel, to the Virgin Mary:

"Behold, thou shalt conceive in thy womb, and bring forth a son, and shalt call His name JESUS. He shall be great, and shall be called the Son of the Most High: and the Lord God shall give unto Him the throne of His father David: and He shall reign over the house of Jacob forever; and of His kingdom there shall be no end" (Luke 1:31-33, R. V.).

It is most significant that during the missionary activities of the nineteenth century, the Gospel of the grace of God that would save the sinner from the consequences of his sin through the regenerating power of the spirit of God, was the principal theme of the ambassadors of Christ. This Gospel of the grace of God was proclaimed unto Joseph by "an angel of the Lord," saying:

"Joseph, thou son of David, fear not to take unto thee Mary thy wife: for that which is conceived in her is of the Holy Spirit. And she shall bring forth a son; and thou shalt call His name Jesus; for it is He that shall save His people from their sins" (Matt. 1:20, 21, R. V.).

Missionaries as Heralds of "The Gospel of the Kingdom."

But, with the opening up of this twentieth century, the missionaries of the Cross began strongly to emphasize in their messages the return of the Messiah to the throne of David. And, through them, "the Gospel of the kingdom" as well as "the Gospel of the grace of God" has been "preached in the whole world for a testimony unto all the nations." Witness, if you will, the wonderful testimony to the Gospel of the kingdom proclaimed by such great missionary organizations as the China Inland Mission, the African Inland Mission, the Christian and Missionary Alliance Missions, and scores of others, denominational and undenominational, whose testimony is ever unequivocally on the side of the good news of a coming Lord to reign on David's throne. We know of no nation "in the whole world" where that "testimony" has not been given. By radio, by word of mouth, by the printed page, the "good news" of the imminency of the coming kingdom has gone forth to all the world. And *this* has not been before. Whether the nations have believed that testimony or not, the testimony has been given. The sign has been fulfilled. And Jesus said, when this is done, *"then* shall the end come!"

Will He keep His promise? We believe He will!

XIII. The "Chariots With Flaming Torches" in Which Men Ride in This Our Day.

"The sure word of prophecy" relates it:

> *"The chariots shall be with flaming torches in the day of His preparation, and the fir trees shall be terribly shaken. The chariots shall rage in the streets, they shall justle one against another in the broad ways: they shall seem like torches, they shall run like the lightnings"* (Nahum 2:3, 4).

The simplest child, reading these words, would have but one vision—*the automobile!* Stand upon any highway and watch them come as "flaming torches," rushing by "like the lightnings." And the very stuff that causes the lightnings to flash through the heavens enables these modern chariots of men to flash by.

Moreover, when these "chariots as flaming torches" dash forth upon the astonished gaze of men *"the fir trees shall be terribly shaken."* As the fig tree is the symbol of Israel, so the fir tree is the emblem of the Gentile nations. And these "chariots as flaming torches," converted into implements of war, are at this moment shaking the fir trees—*"terribly"!*

"They shall justle one against another in the broad ways." Go look at your fenders! And it was the prophet's clear declaration that when these "flaming chariots" appear on earth, "the day of His [our Lord's] preparation" to take over the reins of government on this earth is at hand! In that day we are to——

> *"Behold upon the mountains the feet of Him that bringeth good tidings, that publisheth peace"* (Nah. 1:15).

Oh, how this poor old world longs for the Bringer of "good tidings"— for the Publisher of peace!   Yes, the night cometh! *But also the morning!*

XIV. Mighty Empires of "Clay" Are Crumbling Before Mighty Empires of "Iron" Almost Overnight.

A scene such as this world has never witnessed before. And, the end is not yet!

"The Times of the Gentiles."

Nebuchadnezzar, the mighty Babylonian monarch, dreamed a dream. That dream was history, pre-written by the God Who sees the end from the beginning. It was the narration of that which the Lord Jesus Christ Himself designated as "the times of the Gentiles." "The times of the Gentiles" were those times in which the heel of Gentile power and dominion should gall the neck of the nation of Israel. "Jerusalem shall be trodden down of the Gentiles until the times of the Gentiles be fulfilled" (Luke 21:24).

Those times began with Nebuchadnezzar, who took dominion from Israel; and, will close with the coming of the Son of David from heaven to "have dominion," not only in Jerusalem, but "from sea to sea and from the river unto the ends of the earth. . . . Yea, all kings shall fall down before Him: all nations shall serve Him" (Psalm 72:8-11).

"The times of the Gentiles" were set forth in that image as running their course through four mighty empires. Babylon was represented by the head of gold. Medo-Persia was represented by the arms and breast of silver. Greece was represented by the belly and thighs of brass. Rome was represented by the legs, feet, and toes of iron.

"The Fourth Kingdom"—Rome.

We are concerned today with "the fourth kingdom." This kingdom also was of especial interest to Daniel. (See Daniel 7:19).

The two great iron "legs" imaged the two historic divisions

of the Roman Empire—Constantinople being the capital of the eastern "leg," and Rome being the capital of the western "leg."

The "ten toes" imaged the Roman Empire in its final form— that Empire as it shall exist when "the Stone of Israel" (Gen. 49:24. *Cf.* Dan. 2:34) shall crash down upon it from out of the heavens. With these "toes" we are especially concerned in this momentous hour in which we live.

Now, as we have seen in a previous exposition of this great revelation, the "toes" form an integral part of the "fourth kingdom." All of which means the Roman Empire must be extant when "the Stone" shall fall.

"The Fourth Kingdom" Shall Be Divided.

And, the "ten toes" portray that at the last, the Roman Empire shall exist in a divided, yet unified form. The plain statement of the prophet is: "The kingdom shall be divided" (Dan. 2:41). These "ten toes" typify the last kings who will be on the stage before "the God of heaven [shall] set up a kingdom" (Dan. 2:44). These "toes" symbolize the same kings that the "ten horns" of Daniel 7:24 set forth. And the "ten horns" on the "beast" seen by Daniel are the same "ten horns" the Revelator saw upon the "beast" of his Patmos vision: "I saw a beast . . . having . . . ten horns (Rev. 13:1). And the ten-horned "beast" of Revelation XIII is the ten-horned "beast" of Revelation XVII:

"And the ten horns which thou sawest are ten kings, which have received no kingdom as yet; but receive power as kings one hour with the beast. These shall make war with the Lamb, and the Lamb shall overcome them: for He is Lord of lords, and King of kings" (Rev. 17:12-14).

The statement is so clear and plain that there is scarcely any chance for a mistake of interpretation: *"The ten horns out of this kingdom are ten kings that shall arise"* (Dan. 7:24). And these "ten kings that shall arise" are the "toes," that is, *the extreme end of the image.* Doubtless, the events are now taking place that will compel the final formation of this very federation. These events we will review later.

"Ten Toes"—"Part of Iron and Part of Clay."

"The toes of the feet were part of iron and part of clay, so the kingdom will be partly strong and partly broken" (Dan. 2:43). We are not to understand that the "iron" and the "clay" were fused into one mass. The "iron" kings will be iron. The "clay" kings will be clay. Therefore, some of these kingdoms will be "strong." Some will be "miry," or (marg.) "brittle." The "clay" will crumble before the "iron."

It is generally accepted among nearly all schools of interpreters that the "clay" here symbolizes democracy, while the "iron" symbolizes autocracy. We accept this interpretation. "And whereas thou sawest iron mixed with miry clay, they shall mingle themselves with the seed of men: but they shall not cleave one to another, even as iron is not mixed with clay" (Dan. 2:43). "Iron is not mixed with clay"; that is, "iron" and "clay," like law and grace, are unmixable. Autocrats and "the seed of men" (proletarians) certainly "cleave" *not* "one to another."

The "Ten Toes" Now Appearing.

Draw a line around the Roman Empire when it reached its utmost glory in that long ago, and see how many modern nations lie within. *"More* than ten," you say. Very well. But we are living in days when kingdoms are disappearing overnight. Witness Albania and Poland. When the Antichrist shall have reached the zenith of his career, after the removal of the born-again saints from this earth, there will be exactly *ten!* "The scriptures cannot be broken."

Can we count more than eleven or twelve "toes," at most, at this hour? England, Belgium, France, Portugal, Spain, Switzerland, Italy, Greece, Yugoslavia, Bulgaria, Turkey, and possibly Holland,—these are the now existing *sovereign* states within that old Empire. But even as we write, some of these "sovereign states" are in chains! None but God could have looked down across the sands of twenty-five centuries, and have seen in an Empire then yet unborn, its division into sovereign states today! Talk about an inspired Bible! It is only monumental ignorance that cries out: *"I don't believe!"*

Study the map. Then note the "clay"—representative governments—democracies—where men are supposed to be free. Spain—several years ago—a democracy. The "iron" crashed against it. It crumpled like a leaf. The "iron" stands. The "clay" has passed away. Germany today is "iron," though not "iron" dug from the bowels of the Roman Empire. France—pure "clay"—the foremost representative of democracy. The "iron" crashed the "clay," and—*what have you?*

What About England?

This is a rather foreboding prophecy for England. Even as we write, the German "beast" is vomiting destruction and death upon the cities and towns of Britain. But I didn't write the prophecy. Prophecy was not written to meet my personal desires. I, the democrat, have no love for the autocrat. God's Word, however, must stand! But—thank God—because God's Word stands, I have the assurance that Hitler's dream is only a dream! It is not German "iron," but *Roman* "iron," that will crumble the British "clay," if we interpret the 11th chapter of Daniel correctly. But that picture is still ahead of us.

The "iron" mogul, *out of* Rome, is to "stretch forth his hand also upon the countries: and *the land of Egypt shall not escape*. But he shall have power over the treasures of gold and of silver, and over all the precious things of Egypt" (Dan. 11:42, 43). That is bad news for Britain. I like it not. But "God hath spoken!" The autocrat shall reign. But his reign will be brief. "He shall come to his end and none shall help him" (Dan. 11:45).

Roman "iron" and British "clay" stand face to face today. And the tide of battle moves toward Egypt! More anon! "Iron" and "clay" are colliding today. Finally, the "iron" of autocracy, being "strong," shall prevail. Yes, it shall prevail, but not against "the Stone!" That "Stone of Israel" is a diamond! "Iron" will prove to be as unedurable as "clay" when that "Stone" falls and grinds!

Mankind stands aghast at what is taking place in Europe. We rub our eyes. We stagger, as if waking from some terrible dream. France, with "the finest army in Europe," with her "absolutely impregnable Maginot line," crumbled like brittle "clay" indeed, as the "iron" Juggernaut rolled over and ground her to powder before an amazed and stupefied world. The world should have been reading Daniel. It would have understood. And, there are still some things this old world could learn from Daniel, if it would only turn away from the wisdom of men unto the wisdom that cometh from above.

It would learn that the "iron" will scarcely have crushed the "clay" before "the Stone of Israel" shall come crashing down out of the opened heavens, to break *"in pieces the iron, the brass, the clay, the silver, and the gold"* (Dan. 2:45). And when the powdered dust of Gentile dominion and glory shall have gone with the winds into eternal oblivion, then *"the kingdom and dominion, and the greatness of the kingdom under the whole heaven, shall be given to the people of the saints of the most High, whose kingdom is an everlasting kingdom, and all dominions shall serve and obey Him. Hitherto is the end of the matter"* (Dan. 7:27, 28).

Amen!

XV. The World-Wide Outcry of the Proletarian, and the "Weeping" and "Howling" of the Capitalist—as It Falls Upon Our Ears Today.

"Go to now, ye rich men, weep and howl for your miseries that shall come upon you. Your riches are corrupted, and your garments are motheaten. Your gold and silver is cankered; and the rust of them shall be a witness against you, and shall eat your flesh as it were fire. Ye have heaped treasure together for the last days. Behold, the hire of the labourers who have reaped down your fields, which is of you kept back by fraud, crieth: and the cries of them which have reaped are entered into the ears of the

*Lord of sabaoth. Ye have lived in pleasure on the earth,
and been wanton; ye have nourished your hearts, as in a
day of slaughter"* (James 5:1-5).

The astonishing and unparalleled accumulation of riches on
the part of individuals, made possible by our modern corporations, trusts, and other heaping together of heaps of gold,
taken in connection with the outcry of the whole proletarian
world which feels (rightly or wrongly) that it has been robbed
of its just share in return for the sweat of its brow, is a matter
of common knowledge. "Ye have heaped treasure together
for the last days"—and never before in the history of men
have such stupendous heaps of treasure, heaps upon heaps,
been collected together for the control of the sources of pro-
duction. While it is true that accumulated wealth is essential
in creating employment by turning the wheels of industry,
yet too often the manipulation of these great combinations of
wealth is intended to serve only the selfish purposes of certain
capitalists themselves, and has resulted in an outcry of the
reapers against the heapers such as has never before "entered into the ears of the Lord of sabaoth."

"The Saddest Words in This Generation."

It has not been so long, as the years come and go, that a
young man, then heir to the vastest fortune in America, stood
before the students of Brown University and uttered what
Dr. Newell Dwight Hillis, then the famous liberal pastor of
Plymouth Church, Brooklyn, called "the saddest words in this
generation." In defense of the great trusts, this heir to vast
riches said:

"The American Beauty rose can be produced in all its
splendor only by sacrificing the early buds that grow up
around it. The rose has 1,000 buds, and to produce the
American Beauty the gardener goes around it with a knife and
snips 999, that all the strength and beauty may be forced into
one bloom."

This was the economic argument in favor of corporate
wealth of the corrupt and merciless kind.

Two Kinds of Corporations.

There are, of course, great corporations of an entirely different character, righteously conducted and a blessing to mankind. But great corrupt corporations have fostered the upbuilding of gigantic, autocratic, merciless, and corrupt labor organizations, and beyond them the socialistic and bolshevistic political structures that are threatening the capitalistic world today. The evidence accumulates that these so-called "proletarian" movements quickly develop an autocracy more cruel, bloody, and destructive of human liberty and of the material and spiritual values that make life worth while than corporate wealth has ever done. Proletarianism and capitalism may be equally selfish, but even unrighteous corporate wealth is more fearful and cautious than the proletarian mob. Verily, the problem of a just distribution of the fruits of the earth seems to be beyond the power of unregenerate men to solve, and must await the coming of the "rod out of the stem of Jesse," Who, sitting on "the throne of His father David," "shall not judge after the sight of His eyes, neither reprove after the hearing of His ears: but with righteousness shall He judge the poor, and *reprove with equity* for the meek of the earth" (Isa. 11:1, 3, 4). In His days "they shall build houses and inhabit them; and they shall plant vineyards, and eat the fruit of them. They shall not build and another inhabit; they shall not plant and another eat" (Isa. 65:21, 22). In that day, every man shall possess all he produces, and no man shall live by the sweat of another man's brow.

Heaps upon Heaps.

The Treasury Department of our Government revealed that in the twelve months' period ending December 31, 1928, twenty-four individuals in the United States of America reported a total net income of $242,236,796, or an average of more than $10,000,000 each! Conceive the vastness of that sum if you can—*ten thousand thousand dollars!* And remember, that colossal sum went into the pockets of twenty-four individuals in a single year—supermillionaires indeed!

Moreover, seventeen others reported incomes of from $4,000,-
000 to $5,000,000 each; twenty others with incomes of more
than $3,000,000 and less than $4,000,000 each; and eighty-
nine persons with more than $2,000,000 but less than $3,000,-
000 each; and 346 persons with more than $1,000,000 and
less than $2,000,000 each. All told, 496 persons had an in-
come of more than $1,000,000 each in that year. The total
income of these 496 persons was $1,073,000,000, or an average
of more than *two thousand thousand* dollars each.

Such a heaping of wealth into the hands of a few men and
women, this world has never known before; and, probably never
will know again. And whether unrighteous corporate wealth
was to blame for the debacle of 1929 or not, the fact confronts us that that year of heaping the heaps saw the sacks
of the rich bulge as they never before had bulged, and brought
on the bread lines which encircled the earth in the early '30's.
In this year of 1940, eleven million men are "looking for
work," and twenty million human beings in the most favored
nation of earth are subsisting upon "relief"! And the com-
plaint of the "laborers who have reaped down your fields," ye
rich, are crying out against your "cankered" and "rusted"
wealth. Is it not the fulfillment of the famous prophecy of the
apostle James?

Riches Heaped to Rust—That Is Sin!

In a few outstanding instances, those to whom God has
given great riches have proved by their deeds that they are
conscious that God has entrusted the power of great wealth
to them, and have used the power of riches for temporal and
eternal human good. Blessings be upon their memory! There
is no sin in being rich. If so, why did God make Abraham
and a great line of His choicest Old Testament saints rich?
But riches that are left to "canker" and "rust" in a world
filled with sorrow and want—*that* is sin! And it has also
happened too often that men who became rich through corporate organization, while they used their great riches for
other than personal structures, nevertheless gave their riches
to religious or semi-religious organizations that propagated un-

belief in the inspired Bible and in the necessity of blood atonement for sin, and, therefore, for Satan's kingdom and not the Kingdom of God.

The Foolish Rich.

Again, many of those into whose hands great riches fell were foolish enough to make spectacles of themselves as for the "day of slaughter." We read of the daughter of one of these supermillionaires appearing on the beach of a certain resort in a one-piece bathing suit of tailored ermine valued at $25,000; of "six men interested in things historic and literary" at a dinner in a leading hotel in Philadelphia which cost $2,000 a plate; of a Paris woman paying $1,000 a pair for her stockings; of "Little Villa," a Chihuahua dog valued at more than $1,000 a pound, which was laved in perfume and soap-suds at a cost of $15 for each frequent operation, slept at night "deep-pillowed in silks and scented down," and had his superfluous fat removed at $50 an ounce; and of a college girl spending $3,000 a year for her clothing; etc., etc., etc. At the same time, in the same news columns, we read of all Europe being on short rations; and in the world of men, millions starved or on the verge of starvation.

Susan Lawrence, labor chairman and parliamentary secretary to the Minister of Health in the MacDonald Cabinet (British) stood before the League of Nations Assembly in Geneva a few years ago and said:

"We have sat here day after day hearing delegates from one country after another tell of the miserable state to which their populations have been reduced. There has not been one word of hope nor one real concrete suggestion for a remedy. . . . This . . . [is a matter] of primary importance to the whole population of this planet."

But the "remedy" has not yet been found. Meanwhile, in Russia, the "rich" have been stood up against the walls and shot. And in other lands, the owners of "cankered" and "rusted" treasure heaps have been heard to "weep and howl." Face to face with world revolution, and face to face with an

approaching famine that ex-President Hoover says bids fair
to be the greatest in human history, and in the full knowledge
of what a world revolution means in which famine gnaws at
the vitals of great proletarian hordes, the rich men of earth,
whether guilty or innocent of selfish greed, may well "weep
and howl for the miseries" that will be theirs.

But if those days are upon us, again the clouds are silver-
lined:

*"Be ye also patient; stablish your hearts: for the coming
of the Lord draweth nigh"* (James 5:8).

XIII

THE TRANSLATION OF THE SAINTS

The Two Phases of Christ's Return.

THE longer I live, and the more I meditate upon the revelation of God to man, the more I am convinced of the cor-
rectness of that interpretation of the Scriptures which sets
forth two distinct phases in the return of our Lord from the
heavens.

First, the coming of our Lord Jesus Christ to remove from
the world His born-again ones, even as He removed Enoch
and Elijah—an event known among premillennial students as
The Rapture.

> "Oh, joy! oh, delight! should we go without dying,
> No sickness, no sadness, no dread and no crying;
> Caught up through the clouds with the Lord into glory,
> When Jesus receives 'His own.' "

Second, the coming of the Lord Jesus Christ with His saints
(Jude 14, 15; Rev. 19:14; Zech. 14:3, 5) to judge the nations and to establish the kingdom of the heavens upon the
earth—an event known among all Bible students as *The
Revelation.*

To fail to make a clear distinction between these two events leaves only a confused mind, causing the seeker after truth to throw up his hands in despair, and ofttimes to say:

"I wish I could understand these things! But I just can't! To me, the Scriptures seem so contradictory. For instance, I read in several places in my Bible where Jesus is to come 'as a thief in the night.' [See I Thess. 5:2; II Pet. 3:10; Rev. 3:3; 16:15]. Then I read in another place that when He comes again, 'every eye shall see Him.' [See Rev. 1:7]. It seems to me that it would be a very poor thief that *every eye would see!*"

We agree that such a thief would not get very far with his thievery. But the trouble is, this dear soul fails to distinguish between the *Rapture*, when the children of God shall steal away with Jesus, disappearing suddenly from the haunts of men as if abducted by a thief, and, the *Revelation*, when Christ shall leap forth in majesty from the opened heavens (Rev. 19:11), and "every eye shall see Him."

Between the Rapture and the Revelation.

Between the Rapture (*i.e.*, the coming of Christ *for* His saints) and the Revelation (*i.e.*, the coming of Christ *with* His saints) events of tremendous interest take place. Outstanding among these events we note:

1. The revelation of the Antichrist (II Thess. 2:8) and his rise to the zenith of his power and glory.

2. "Ten kings," within the confines of the historic Roman Empire, entering into an agreement to federate their kingdoms with the Antichrist at the head of this great confederacy—the Roman Empire in its final form.

3. The refusal of the Jews to deify and to worship this new world god (the born-again saints will have gone into the heavens), who, Nebuchadnezzar-like, will then seek their extermination (Rev. 13:15). This will be "the time of Jacob's trouble" foretold by Jeremiah the prophet (30:4-7), even "the great tribulation" foretold by Christ (Matt. 24:21). In those days, supernatural judgments will be poured out upon the whole Gentile world, even as it is written: "Behold, the Lord cometh out of His place to punish the inhabitants of the earth for their

iniquity" (Isa. 26:20, 21). *"Great tribulation"* for the Jews, and *great "indignation"* (Dan. 11:36; Zeph. 3:8) for the Gentiles! These judgments are described in detail in the book of the Revelation, chapters six to nineteen.

4. The return of Elijah and another prophet, probably Enoch, to save Israel from complete destruction by the Antichrist, and to prepare a remnant among them for the coming of their Messiah (Mal. 14:5, 6; Rev. 11:3-6).

5. The judgment of Satanically inspired ecclesiasticism—the great harlot (Rev. 17).

6. The judgment of Gog and his allies (Ezek. 38 and 39).

7. The "war of Armageddon," culminating in the overthrow of the Antichrist and all his hosts (Rev. 16:14-16, R. V.; Joel 3:1-17; Dan. 11:36-45; 12:1; Rev. 19:11-21).

The period of time between the *Rapture* and the *Revelation*, during which these events take place, is believed by careful Bible students to be a period of seven years. This they glean from a study of Daniel's great prophecy of "the seventy weeks" (Dan. 9:24-27). Daniel was told that "seventy weeks" (literally, "seventy sevens" of years) "are determined *upon thy people"*—the Jews. Sixty-nine of those sevens of years ended with the "Messiah [being] cut off" (Dan. 9:25). Christ was crucified exactly 483 (sixty-nine sevens) years after "the going forth of the commandment to restore and to build Jerusalem" (Dan. 9:25. *Cf.* Neh. 2:5, 6).

After the rejection of Christ by Israel on that momentous day when He came riding down the brow of old Olivet (Luke 19:28-44), offering the kingdom to Israel by every possible token, the Church was brought into being as the organism through which God would continue His work upon the earth. When the Church is caught away into the heavens, God will again deal with Israel, and the seventieth seven of years will have its fulfillment. Daniel's great prophecy of "seventy weeks" is one of the highest "mountain peaks of prophecy," and nothing short of a volume can do it full justice.* Other

---

* To the reader who may wish to make a study of this most important prophecy, we commend a study of the booklet, *"The Seventy Weeks of Daniel,"* (Price 35¢) by Dr. Alva J. McClain, President of Grace Theological Seminary, Winona Lake, Ind.

passages throw light also upon the probable length of time between the two great phases of our Lord's appearing, such as Rev. 11:6, 14, and 13:5. But here we must leave it now.

The Rapture.

It is our purpose here to deal with the Rapture—that blessed hope for which all true and well-informed children of God are now standing on tiptoe with glorious expectancy. Every sign of the times, even as we have seen, indicates that it is, indeed, an imminent hope.

> "Perhaps, today, shall sound the mystic summons;
> The shout! the voice! the trump! not by all heard:
> And, from their scattered, silent resting places,
> The dead in Christ will rise to meet the Lord;
> While we, the ransomed living, in a moment
> Shall be 'caught up',—according to His Word."

On the eve of the darkest day that this earth has ever seen, the Lord Jesus informed His disciples that "His hour was come that He should depart out of this world" (John 13:1). They were utterly dismayed and heart-broken. Jesus immediately comforted them with a precious promise that, through many a dark day, buoyed the drooping spirits of the saints:

> "Let not your heart be troubled: ye believe in God, believe also in Me. In My Father's house are many mansions: if it were not so I would have told you. I go to prepare a place for you. And if I go and prepare a place for you, I will come again, and receive you unto Myself; that where I am, there ye may be also" (John 14:1-3).

"I will come again!" But *how* will He "come again"?

"Unto the church of the Thessalonians" the apostle Paul gave a crystalline clear description of the glorious fulfillment of this promise of Christ. We cannot tell it more simply or more plainly than it is written:

> "But I would not have you to be ignorant, brethren, concerning them which are asleep, that ye sorrow not, even as others which have no hope.

"For if we believe that Jesus died and rose again, even so them also which sleep in Jesus will God bring with Him.

"For this we say unto you by the word of the Lord, that we which are alive and remain unto the coming of the Lord shall not prevent (R.V., *precede*) them which are asleep.

"For the Lord Himself shall descend from heaven with a shout, with the voice of the archangel, and with the trump of God: and the dead in Christ shall rise first:

"Then we which are alive and remain shall be caught up together with them in the clouds, to meet the Lord in the air: and so shall we ever be with the Lord.

"Wherefore comfort one another with these words" (I Thess. 4:13-18).

Christian, is it thinkable that our Lord would tell us to "comfort one another with these words," if "these words" cannot be clearly understood? Would the infinitely wise God "speak into the air"—a fault that He so seriously condemned in others? (See I Cor. 14:6-12). No! The plain fact is, that "Jesus [Who] died and rose again," some day soon is going to "descend from heaven" and with a mighty "shout" call for the righteous dead to arise. *And they will rise!* One day He stood at the tomb of Lazarus and cried: "Lazarus, come forth!" And Lazarus came forth. It is well that He named Lazarus. Otherwise, every sleeper in the tombs of the earth might have gotten up. In the first resurrection, only the righteous dead arise (*Cf.* Rev. 20:5, 6); for it is written that when the voice of His trumpet sounds, "the dead in Christ shall rise *first.*"

Then—*what?* "*Then* we that are alive and remain shall be caught up together with them to meet the Lord in the air." No airplanes will be needed. No, not even the wings of a dove. Spiritual bodies will not be subject to natural laws.

But a certain great "change" must take place before "we that are alive"—we that, like Enoch (Heb. 11:5), will not have seen death—can be "caught up to meet the Lord in the air." It is written:

"Now this I say, brethren, that flesh and blood cannot inherit the kingdom of God; neither doth corruption inherit incorruption. Behold, I shew you a mystery; We shall not all sleep, but *we shall all be changed,* in a moment, in the twinkling of an eye, at the last trump: for the trumpet shall sound, and the dead shall be raised incorruptible, and *we shall be changed"* (I Cor. 15:50-52).

Two things are to take place "in the twinkling of an eye." *First,* the saints' bodies that lie corrupted in the graves will be raised, and, by the omnipotent Word that created the heavens and the earth, will instantly "be fashioned like unto His glorious body" (Phils. 3:21). *Then* the saints who have lived to see that day, by that same omnipotent Word *"shall be changed"* to be "like Him." "Beloved, now are we the sons of God, and it doth not yet appear what we shall be; but we know that, when He shall appear, we shall be like Him" (I John 3:2).

Then, when the "dead in Christ" shall have risen, and "we that are alive and remain" shall have been "changed," so that together we can be presented "unto Himself a glorious church, not having spot, or wrinkle, or any such thing" (Hallelujah!), then, the risen ones and the changed ones shall hear His voice calling:

"Thou art all fair, My love; there is no spot in thee. . . . Rise up, My love, My fair one, and come away!" (Song of Sol. 3:7; 2:10).

And up, up, far away from every possible earth stain, whether of tears or of sin, we shall rise into the "mansions" wherein He promised to go and prepare a place for us. The great Bridegroom will never break His plighted faith with His Bride! *He will come!*

"As a Thief in the Night."

He will come "as a thief in the night"—quietly, unobserved, unseen except by the watchers. As for the world, it will be asleep. "For *as a snare* it shall come upon all them that dwell on the face of the whole earth" (Luke 21:35). "I tell you, in that night, there shall be two men in one bed; the one shall be taken, and the other shall be left" (Luke 17:34).

The one was not a watcher for the coming of the Lord. The other was watching, and, therefore, it was his blessed privilege to "steal away with Jesus." "What I say unto you," said Jesus, "I say unto all, Watch!" (Mark 13:37).

And they that watch, "They shall be Mine, said the Lord of hosts, in that day when I make up My jewels" (Mal. 3:17). Verily, for what does a thief come? He comes not for your flat-irons, or your stove-pokers, or your dish rags, or your tin pans, or your garbage pots. The thief comes for your diamonds, your rubies, your pearls—your jewels! What honor—what glory—is ahead for the loyal saints of God! They shall be the jewels of the King of Glory! What grace! What grace! What grace!

Old Testament Revelation of the Rapture.

Old Testament saints shall have part in that translation. If not, when shall they arise? If Old Testament saints are to have a part in that rapture, why should not they have had some revelation of that coming glory? They did have a revelation. We read:

"Thy dead men shall live, together with My dead body shall they arise. Awake and sing, ye that dwell in dust: for thy dew is as the dew of herbs, and the earth shall cast out the dead. Come, My people, enter thou into thy chambers, and shut thy doors about thee: hide thyself as it were for a little moment, until the indignation be overpast. For, behold, the Lord cometh out of His place to punish the inhabitants of the earth for their iniquity: the earth also shall disclose her blood, and shall no more cover her slain" (Isaiah 26:19-21).

What a marvelous portrayal of the whole event.

"The earth shall cast out the dead." This is resurrection, but it is a resurrection of the righteous dead. It is "Thy dead," O God, that shall "awake and sing." The wicked awake only to "weep and howl for the miseries that shall come upon them."

"Together with my dead body shall they arise." "Even so," said Paul, speaking of the same event, "them also which sleep in Jesus will God bring," even as He brought Christ Jesus, from the prison of the dead.

The Trumpet "Shout."

I have often wondered just what our Lord would "shout" through the mighty trumpet that shall awake the righteous dead. I believe the Old Testament revelation of the Rapture gives answer: "*Come, My people*" [and *up* we will go], "enter thou into thy chambers [even the "mansions"], and shut thy doors about thee: hide thyself for a little moment, until the indignation be overpast."

"The indignation" as we have seen, is a well defined period of time. Daniel said that the willful king (the Antichrist) "shall prosper until *the indignation* be accomplished" (Dan. 11:36). Isaiah did not leave us in doubt as to what this "indignation" means: "*Behold, the Lord* cometh out of His place, to punish the inhabitants of the earth for their iniquity: the earth also shall disclose her blood, and shall no more cover her slain" (Isaiah 26:21). That means judgment! Terrible, terrible judgment!

Can any one doubt, in the face of these assurances from the infallible Word of God, that the children of God will escape those awful days in which the Antichrist shall reign and when God's terrible judgments shall fall upon a Christ-rejecting world?

"Watch ye therefore, and pray always, that ye may be accounted worthy to escape all these things that shall come to pass, and to stand before the Son of man" (Luke 21:36).

"Worthy?" Yes, worthy because in His own precious blood He will have cleansed us from having "spot, or wrinkle, or any such thing"! When my precious daughter, Iva, was lying at the gates to glory, she called her only brother, Paul—a minister of the Gospel—to her bedside and gave to him the last message he was ever to receive from his only sister: "Remember, Paul, nothing but the precious blood of Jesus can ever make us worthy!" What better message for a young minister of the Gospel in these times of terrible apostasy!

Years ago, a little baby seal appeared at the foot of the pier here in the city of Long Beach. It was lost. For days it played about in the water's edge. Tourists flocked to watch it, and to feed it. It became quite tame. Then, one day, far out on the sea, a head appeared above the water and a peculiar cry was heard. Instantly that little seal, hearing that voice and knowing it, "turned tail" and disappeared, to be seen no more! The mother had found her own!

"Rise up, My love, My fair one, and come away." When that voice calls, we shall know and we shall go! The great Shepherd will have found His own!

XIV

THE WAR OF ARMAGEDDON

"*Thud! thud! .Thud! thud!*
Myriads of heavy feet pound and shuffle in the dust;
Myriads of war-plagued men,
Jaded soldiers, haggard-eyed, heavy-laden shoulders sagging,
Marching to the wars again;
Endless miles and endless marching, through the rain
And through the mud;
On the road again to ruin, marching with their ceaseless
Thud! thud! .Thud! thud!

"*Thud! thud! .Thud! thud!*
Heavy boots upon the highway pass the shattered wayside
trees;
Hurry through the shell-wracked town;
Past the gaunt uprearing ruins, cottage, market place and
mansion,
Windows staring blindly down.
Plodding feet in straggling columns, trudging over war-torn
ground,
Lately drenched with crimson blood,
Toward the futile Armageddon; marching with their endless
Thud! thud! .Thud! thud!"

THUS wrote Ralph Mitchell Crosby in 1939, as the goose-stepping legions of Germany began their hell-bent march once again, over the ground upon which the rivers of blood had scarcely dried up from the ghastly butcheries of 1914-1918. "Thud, thud! Thud, thud!" But is it *"Toward Armageddon,"* as Mr. Crosby captioned his verses? We do not doubt it!

But, I cannot agree with Mr. Crosby that it is "toward the *futile* Armageddon." Verily, when the steamy blood vapors shall have cooled above Armageddon's crimson ground, the only war ever to be truly the death of war will have been fought, and the nations of the earth "shall beat their swords into plowshares, and their spears into pruninghooks: [and] nation shall not lift up sword against nation, neither shall they learn war any more" (Isa. 2:4). That result will not be "futile"!

Armageddon, a War.

Contrary to the popular idea, Armageddon is a *war,* rather than a "battle." We read in the Revelation (16:14-16) of the day when the "spirits of devils . . . go forth unto the kings of the earth and of the whole world, to gather them to the *battle* of that great day of God Almighty . . . into a place called in the Hebrew tongue Armageddon." From that Scripture apparently has come the expression—*"the battle of Armageddon."* But the *Revised Version* gives us the better translation—*"the war of Armageddon."* Yes, the Armageddon toward which the delusioned goose-steppers of the earth are thudding their way is a *war—a series of battles.* It is doing no violence to the truth, however, to speak of *the last battle* of "the war of Armageddon," as *"the battle* of Armageddon." Upon the outcome of this last battle of the war of Armageddon, the hope of all the future depends.

No Scripture gives us a clearer understanding of the cause and the course of this war of Armageddon than does Daniel, chapter eleven. If we link together this chapter with Joel, chapter 3, and Revelation, chapter 19, the Biblical narrative of the world's last round of agony will be just about complete.

We have sometimes heard Bible teachers speak of "the wars of the Antichrist." Why not speak of "the war of Armaged-

don," with the Antichrist as the leader of the hosts on one side
of the forces engaged in each of its battles? I believe that
would be more definite. With this understanding, we can begin to follow the campaigns of Satan's superman with the
divine record in Daniel 11:36:

> "And the king shall do according to his will; and he
> shall exalt himself, and magnify himself above every god,
> and shall speak marvellous things against the God of gods,
> and shall prosper till the indignation be accomplished: for
> that that is determined shall be done" (Dan. 11:36).

The Antichrist, the Leader of the Satanic Hosts.

No one who reads this passage in the light of the other
Scriptures that clearly describe the Antichrist can see in this
willful king any personage other than the Antichrist. The
description fits perfectly into the picture of the Antichrist
drawn by Paul (I Thess. 2:3, 4) and by John (Rev. 13:4-8).
In all three of these passages we find the Antichrist to be a
personage who

1. Is energized by Satan;
2. Blasphemes the God of Israel;
3. Deifies himself and exalts himself "above every God";
and, who
4. "Prospers" during a brief period of time, even "the indignation."

A Solemn Warning Against Deception.

The Antichrist is the false messiah who, riding forth on a
"white horse . . . conquering and to conquer" (Rev. 6:2),
will imitate the real Messiah, Who shall return to earth astride
a "white horse" to tread "the winepress of the fierceness and
wrath of Almighty God" (Rev. 19:11,15). Satan's imitation
of the matchless Christ will deceive the unregenerate sons of
Israel, even as Jesus declared: "I am come in My Father's
name, and ye receive Me not: if another shall come in his own
name, him ye will receive" (John 5:43). Jesus, therefore, issued this clear warning:

"*Then* if any shall say unto you, Lo, here is Christ, or there; believe it not. . . . Behold, I have told you before. Wherefore, if they shall say unto you, Behold, He is in the desert; go not forth: behold, He is in the secret chambers; believe it not. For as the lightning cometh out of the east, and shineth even unto the west; so shall also the coming of the Son of man be" (Matt. 24:23-27).

One thing sure, those who take Christ at His word, and will accept none as Savior except the One Who shall ride forth, *personally and visibly* out of the heaven above, will not be deceived by any false Christ arising up from the earth! They will never "worship the beast" nor receive his mark (Rev. 13:8, 15, 16).

The Willful King, the Head of the Roman Empire.

As I have so often set forth on these pages, the Antichrist will appear as the ten-horned beast of Daniel's dream and John's vision. He will become the head of the Roman Empire in its final form, when God will put into the hearts of the ten Mediterranean powers "to fulfil his will, and to agree, and give their kingdom unto the beast, until the words of God shall be fulfilled" (Rev. 17:17).

The Foes of the Antichrist.

Daniel clearly sets forth the fact that this willful king (Dan. 11:36) will begin his last campaign wedged in between two mighty foes.

First, *"at the time of the end shall the king of the south push at him"* (Dan. 11:40).

Thus the war of Armageddon shall begin. And who is "the king of the south"? The expression, "the south," can be applied, and has been applied, to various portions of the earth's surface—and properly so. To have real meaning here in Daniel, we must ask—*"south"* of what? The prophecy is concerned with the land of Israel—the land of Daniel's "people" (Dan. 9:24). "The king of the south" must be some king whose influence and whose possessions predominate in the countries *south* of "the middle of the earth" (Ezek. 38:12, R. V.).

Only Great Britain, in these last days, can fit into the picture. Britain it is whose territories and whose great political influence sweep from the North Sea down to Gibraltar's sturdy "Rock," on through Egypt, the Red Sea, Arabia, India, Burmah, Indo-China, and around to the warm seas of Japan—a mighty semicircle stretching across the whole of the Eastern Hemisphere, around Jerusalem at its center. Other nations may have possessions along that route; but it is Britain that is vastly predominant. And, of course, in the Biblical picture we must include the allies of Britain.

Second, *"And the king of the north shall come against him like a whirlwind"* (Dan. 11:40).

What "king" is it whose dominions sweep in a vast semicircle around Jerusalem, to the north, from the icy waters of the Baltic to within a mile of our own American shores—a mighty territory taking in about one-sixth of the land surface of the earth? It is Russia! Russia is "the king of the north" —Russia and Russia's end-time allies, even "Gomer," "Togarmah," etc., (*Cf.* Ezek. 38:5, 6, R. V.).

The Antichrist, vs. Great Britain.

It is apparent that the war of Armageddon begins with "the king of the south" pushing at the willful king—the Antichrist —in the beginning of his swift rise to power. This fact makes the present strife between Italy and Great Britain of most intense interest. For many years the author has said that when the Antichrist shall come and begin his activities, war between Italy and Great Britain will ensue. We have based this belief chiefly on the following statement from the prophet Daniel:

> "He shall stretch forth his hand also upon the countries: and the land of Egypt shall not escape. But he shall have power over the treasures of gold and of silver, and over all the precious things of Egypt: and the Libyans and the Ethiopians shall be at his steps" (Dan. 11:42, 43).

It should be patent to all that the Antichrist, a Roman prince, could never secure "power . . . over all the precious things of Egypt" until he has first brought Great Britain, protector of Egypt, to her knees. I have always said that "Daniel 11 contains discomfiting news for Great Britain!" However, it is not Berlin, but Rome, that will benefit by Britain's discomfit.

The Line of March.

"He shall enter also into the glorious land, and many shall be overthrown" (Dan. 11:41). With the God of Israel there is only one "glorious land"—the land of Abraham, Isaac, Jacob, and David—the land that was hallowed by the precious blood of His well-beloved Son. When the hour of his destiny arrives, the Antichrist will march his forces into Palestine. The line of march will see "many overthrown." Albania is already gone. Jugoslavia, Greece, Bulgaria, Turkey, Syria, Iraq, and Arabia, are all on or bordering on this highway around the Roman sea from Rome to Egypt. Will some of these, or all of these, fall as the rider on the "white horse" goes "forth conquering and to conquer" (Rev. 6:2)? Time will tell.

Three countries along that line of march, however, even "these shall escape out of his hand, Edom, and Moab, and the chief of the children of Ammon" (Dan. 11:41). And we are not left in the dark for the reason why "these shall escape out of his hand." "These" are the wilderness countries, east of the Jordan, preserved for the persecuted "woman" (Israel) that, in that day, "she might fly into the wilderness, into her place, where she is [to be] nourished for a time, and times, and half a time [three and a half years], from the face of the serpent" (Rev. 12:14). These are the "mountains" our Lord had in mind when He warned of the time of "great tribulation" (Matt. 24:21), "even the time of Jacob's trouble" (Jer. 30:7), and said: "Then let them which be in Judea flee into the mountains" (Matt. 24:16). These wilderness countries will form a refuge for Israel, and into that refuge Israel's God does not permit the conquering hosts of Antichrist to enter as they, avoiding Britain's mighty fleet, march victoriously around the rim of the Mediterranean, from the Tiber to the Nile.

Dictators, Puppets of the Living God.

In those days God's hand will rest heavily upon the nations and He will deliver "many" into the hand of the Antichrist, even as He once delivered "many" into the hand of Nebuchadnezzar. Before Nebuchadnezzar marched, the prophet of God solemnly warned:

> "Therefore thus saith the Lord of hosts; Because ye have not heard My words, Behold, I will send and take all the families of the north, saith the Lord, and Nebuchadnezzar the king of Babylon, My servant, and will bring them against this land, and against the inhabitants thereof, and against all these nations round about, and will utterly destroy them, and make them an astonishment, and a hissing, and perpetual desolations. . . . And this whole land shall be a desolation, and an astonishment; and these nations shall serve the king of Babylon seventy years" (Jer. 25:8, 9, 11).

It should be said here, however, that God did not fail also to prophesy the judgment that fell upon the wicked Nebuchadnezzar himself, when he had fulfilled the purpose of the God Who "maketh the wrath of man to praise Him." For it was also written:

> "And it shall come to pass, when seventy years are accomplished, that I will punish the king of Babylon, and that nation, saith the Lord, for their iniquity, and the land of the Chaldeans, and will make it perpetual desolations" (Jer. 25:12).

Note the significant statement—"this whole land [of Israel] shall be a desolation . . . *seventy years*"; but when "desolations" are visited upon Babylon, they shall be *"perpetual."*

History will repeat itself again. The nations that have scorned the words of God will be given into the hands of the Antichrist, of whom Nebuchadnezzar was a remarkable foreshadow. Unconsciously to himself, the Antichrist will be a "sword" in the hands of Jehovah, and for judgment purposes will perform the will of God, until he himself shall be judged.

Dictators are but pawns in the hands of the God of Israel,

and, consciously or unconsciously, they move to carry out the mysteries of His will. The God still lives who said of Cyrus the Great, more than a hundred years before he was born: *"He is My shepherd, and shall perform all My pleasure: even saying to Jerusalem, Thou shalt be built; and to the temple, Thy foundation shall be laid"* (Isa. 44:28). To one great pagan autocrat, even Nebuchadnezzar, God said: "Go ye, and destroy Jerusalem and the temple therein." Then to another great Gentile autocrat, even Cyrus, He said: "Go build what you, O Gentile, have destroyed!" And the mighty Gentile meekly obeyed! Verily, Nebuchadnezzar, Cyrus, Alexander, Cæsar, Napoleon, Stalin, Mussolini, Hitler—puppets all, of the God of the people they have so despised!

The Conquering Antichrist in Egypt.

When the Antichrist, conquering only within the permissive will of God, shall have arrived in Egypt, he will find, of course, "the Libyans and the Ethiopians at his steps" (Dan. 11:43). Twenty-five centuries ago the prophet of God said it would be so. Today, even so it is!

Several years ago, fifty-two nations clamped down their "sanctions" on the Italian dictator as he started his legions on the march into Ethiopia, and those fifty-two nations leagued together and said, "It shall not be!" But that mattered not! "The scriptures cannot be broken." The Ethiopians joined the Libyans "at his steps." What marvelous fulfillments of the prophecies spoken twenty-five centuries ago, are we witnessing today. Is this book—the Bible—the Word of God? Verily, it is the most ignorant man on the jury who exclaims: "I don't believe!"

Quickly, after his arrival in Egypt, will the treasures and all "the precious things of Egypt" become the possession of the Antichrist. "The king of the south" will lose the battle! But even so, in the purposes of God, the wicked willful king must "prosper till the indignation be accomplished" (Dan. 11:36).

"The Indignation."

"The indignation," as we have already clearly set forth upon these pages, is the divine designation for those days when the judgment of God will rest heavily upon the nations which, either roughly or politely, have bowed Christ out of their councils, and have persecuted His "anointed" earthly people—Israel!   Graphically did the prophet Isaiah portray that time:

> "Thy dead men shall live, together with My dead body shall they arise. Awake and sing, ye that dwell in dust: for thy dew is as the dew of herbs, and the earth shall cast out the dead. Come, My people, enter thou into thy chambers, and shut thy doors about thee: hide thyself as it were for a little moment, until the indignation be overpast. For, behold, the Lord cometh out of His place to punish the inhabitants of the earth for their iniquity: the earth also shall disclose her blood, and shall no more cover her slain" (Isa. 26:19-21).

The Silver Lining in the Cloud.

Thank God, before those awful days when "the indignation" of an outraged God shall rest so heavily upon the nations that the living will be unable to bury the dead, and, "except those days should be shortened, there should no flesh be saved" (Matt. 24:22), the righteous dead will be awakened to put on glory, and, with the changed living saints, shall answer to the sky shout:

> "Come, my people, enter thou into thy chambers, and shut thy doors about thee: hide thyself as it were for a little moment, until the indignation be overpast" (Isa. 26:20. *Cf.* I. Thess. 4:13-18).

The Three Stepping-Stones of the Antichrist to Power.

Let us keep in mind the fact that when the Antichrist shall arise to the zenith of his career, he will have absolute power over all the *economic* forces of the world; for "no man" will be able to "buy or sell, save he that has the mark, or the name of the beast, or the number of his name" (Rev. 13:17). Likewise, he will have absolute power over the *political forces* of the world, for "power" shall be "given him over all kindreds, and tongues, and nations" (Rev. 13:7). And, finally, he will have absolute power over all the *spiritual forces* of the world, for "all that dwell upon the earth shall worship him," and he will "cause that as many as would not worship the image of the beast should be killed" (Rev. 13:8, 15).

In the attainment of this high eminence, this "man of sin" will have used three stepping-stones:

First, "the great whore that sitteth upon many waters" (Rev. 17:1).

Who but Ecclesiastical Rome can be the harlot that appears in the vision our Lord gave to John on Patmos? Who can this harlot be but an apostate church, once the bride of Christ (Eph. 5:31, 32), that departed from her kingly Husband, and went away and "committed fornication" by forming unholy alliances with "the kings of the earth"? (Rev. 17:2).

The union of Church and State before God is spiritual adultery. When the famous revelator "saw a woman sit upon a scarlet colored beast full of names of blasphemy, having seven heads and ten horns" (v. 3), he simply saw "that great city, which reigneth over the kings of the earth," even Ecclesiastical Rome, appearing as having dominant influence over the "beast"—Political Rome—as "the beast" arose to power.

In view of this divine portrayal, it is of intensest interest to watch the machinations of the famous old intriguer in the Vatican. When the first head of the revived Roman Empire (Mussolini) came upon the scene, he paid humble acknowledgment to Papal Rome in more ways than one, even restoring to the "mother of harlots" a temporal state. And ever since, the bejeweled "harlot" has blessed the banners of Rome as those banners floated over the legions who marched forth to the plunder in Ethiopia, in Spain, and in Albania. Let none be deceived by the tears of Papal Rome and her expressed horror of the rivers of blood now flowing in Europe into thinking that there is no secret understanding between Papal Rome and Political Rome today. It is unthinkable that Papal Rome would be blessing the banners of Mussolini's highbinders, when they are joining hands with the Pope-despising goose-steppers of Hitler and the priest-hating assassins of Stalin, if there were no understanding. The crafty old Jesuit understands! The deep-plotting Fascist understands!

Secondly, some great political power, duped into upbearing the Roman into power.

Antiochus Epiphanes is the pattern, according to Daniel the prophet. For the world's last Cæsar "shall come in peaceably," as Mussolini, the Roman head, did come when he marched on Rome in 1922. And the dictator has kept his grip on the Roman Catholic citizenry of Italy very largely "by flatteries" (Dan. 11:21). How his blandiloquous tongue has beslavered Italy now for nearly twenty years about her innate greatness and glory, promising that she is soon to be glorious "as in the days of Augustus Cæsar!" Hitler has used the same method with his German dupes.

Again, as did Antiochus, the Roman, *"After the league made with him, he shall work deceitfully"* (Dan. 11:23). That ought to be interesting reading for Adolf Hitler! We risk repeating a former statement: *Adolf Hitler is due for a great betrayal.* Papal Rome believes *that,* else she would never bless the banners of Benito Mussolini, as her cardinals have done.

Thirdly, the Jew who will certainly play his destined part in exalting the Roman to power; for the Antichrist "shall confirm a covenant with many [of Daniel's people—the Jews] *for one week* [seven years]" (Dan. 9:27).

Just how this will work out in the last hours of Gentile dominion we do not know, but work out it will. What an hour, even now, for some man to get back of him the enormous power of international Jewry by coming to its rescue as the waves of anti-Semitism threaten engulfment! Will this also come with the betrayal of Adolf Hitler? We do know that the Roman Cæsar was extremely friendly to the Jews of Italy until he "made love" to Adolf Hitler. We know also that he has posed as a Jew-baiter in the wooing of Hitler to become his tool for humbling the might of France and England as they barred his way to the fulfillment of his dream of Roman glory. We know also that neither the Italian dictator nor his people are over-zealous in any anti-Semitic program.

The "Ten Kings" Form Their Alliance—In Egypt.

Frequently has our attention been called to the fact that in the deep twilight of "the times of the Gentiles," "ten kings" whose dominions shall be within the boundary lines of the old Roman Empire, shall *"have one mind, and shall give their power and strength unto the beast"* (Rev. 17:13)—even unto the Antichrist.

Now, when "ten kings" together shall surrender their power —their armies and navies, their financial resources and their very destinies—into the hands of a single individual, even for "one hour," there will have to be some absolutely compelling reason therefor.

Bear in mind that the Roman Cæsar will bring "the king of the south"—the mighty Briton—to his knees. If not in complete subjugation, yet the Mediterranean nations will all be at the place where the Roman conqueror will be able to dic-tate the policy of those nations. (Personally, I do not glory in the prospect, but I did not write the Scriptures! My task is to explain them!)

"Tidings" That Trouble "The Beast."

Having arrived at this point, resting a bit on his laurels, while there in Egypt, suddenly he hears some disconcerting news. It is written:

> *"Tidings out of the east, and out of the north shall trou-ble him"* (Dan. 11:44).

What can the distressing "tidings" be? The only revealed answer is to be found in Ezekiel's revelation of the machina-tions of hoary old Gog:

> "Thus saith the Lord God; It shall also come to pass, that at the same time shall things come into thy mind, and thou shalt think an evil thought: And thou shalt say, I will go up to the land of unwalled villages; I will go to

them that are at rest, that dwell safely, all of them dwelling without walls, and having neither bars nor gates. To take a spoil, and to take a prey; to turn thine hand upon the desolate places that are now inhabited, and upon the people that are gathered out of the nations, which have gotten cattle and goods, that dwell in the midst of the land" (Ezek. 38:10-12).

Gog—the great "king of the north"—recent spoiler of Poland, Finland, Latvia, Lithuania, Estonia, and Rumania—for centuries has had his beady old eyes fixed on "the navel of the earth"—Palestine. The warm seaports of southern lands, the enormous riches of the Dead Sea, the oil fields of Iraq and Syria—these have long caused the bloody jaws of old Gog to slobber in streams. And after all, why not? Will not a despised Fascist foe have marched through that land, on into Egypt, to "take a spoil"? Why should the old Bear then hibernate in his den while the Fascist "beast" gobbles up everything in sight? It will be "now or never"! The mighty Gog, with "Gomer" (Germany), "Togarmah," "Persia," "Cush," and "Phut," will mobilize their legions, saddle their vast multitudes of horses, and begin their fatal march down past the cedars of Lebanon. It is written:

"And thou shalt come from thy place out of the north parts, thou, and many people with thee, all of them riding upon horses, a great company, and a mighty army: And thou shalt come up against My people of Israel, as a cloud to cover the land" (Ezek. 38:15-16).

Need anyone ask what the "tidings" shall be that shall trouble the Fascist chief?

While we are not dogmatic on this point, yet we have an idea that we are in the neighborhood of *the absolutely compelling reason* for the quick formation of the "ten kings" into a league that, with the "beast" out of Rome at its head, will bring the Roman Empire to the zenith of its latter day power and glory. It is the Bolshevik specter "out of the north parts" that will make close bedfellows out of the otherwise bitter enemies! We may be pardoned for going beyond that which is actually written long enough to express the opinion that the famous alliance of "ten kings" will be consummated *in Egypt*— an alliance to last for "one hour," or long enough ostensibly to "save civilization" from the savagery of allied Bolshevism and Naziism!

Gog's Enemies Will Become Furious.

When this awful anti-Christ, anti-God, anti-Jew, anti-humanity, anti-civilization, anti-everything-that-is-decent, Bolshevistic, Naziistic horde "out of the north parts" shall begin its descent on "the glorious land," quitclaimed over four thousand years ago by Jehovah to Abraham, then it shall be even as decreed by the God of Abraham, Isaac, and Jacob:

> "My fury shall come up into My face. For, in My jealousy and in the fire of My wrath have I spoken . . . I will call for a sword against him [Gog] throughout all My mountains . . . and I will plead against him with pestilence and with blood; and I will rain upon him, and upon his hands, and upon the many people that are with him, an overflowing rain, and great hailstones, fire, and brimstone" (Ezek. 38:18-22).

Likewise, in Egypt, the victorious rider of the "white horse" (Rev. 6:2), troubled by the mobilization and march of Gog, will become furious, even as it is written:

> *"Therefore he shall go forth with great fury to destroy and to utterly make away many"* (Dan. 11:44).

"Fury" in the face of God! "Fury" in the face of Antichrist! "Fury" in heaven and "fury" in hell—all directed against the godless Gog! There can be only one result!

Jehovah-God Calls for "a Sword."

As the God of Israel called for the sword of Nebuchadnezzar, so He will call for the sword (Ezek. 38:12) of Satan's last-day superman, and direct him to march his allied kings back, out of Egypt, up into "the glorious land" against Gog! What an hour of destiny that will be! God, Who orders all things ac-

cording to the mystery of His will, at last sends Satan forth
for the judgment of the godless hordes of Gog!

The Battle in Esdraelon—The Doom of Gog.

Those satanic legions will meet southeast of old Mount Carmel, in the valley of Esdraelon, where, "by the waters of
Megiddo . . . the stars in their courses fought against Sisera"
(Judges 5:19, 20). The outcome of that last awful saturnalia
of blood, in which Gentile will be arrayed against Gentile, is
vividly delineated by the prophet Ezekiel. Thus saith the
Lord:

> "And it shall come to pass in that day, that I will give
> unto Gog a place there of graves in Israel, the valley of
> the passengers on the east of the sea: and it shall stop
> the noses of the passengers: and there shall they bury
> Gog and all his multitude: and they shall call it The valley
> of Hamon-gog. And seven months shall the house of
> Israel be burying of them, that they may cleanse the land"
> (Ezek. 39:11, 12).

Thus will end the glory of the anti-God goose-steppers from
Berlin and Moscow! Instead of burying the Jew, the Jew will
bury them! Fertilizer will they become for the very land of
the people they have so utterly despised!

The Antichrist Supreme.

But this sanguinary contest between Gentile hordes for the
Gentile dominion of the earth, while a battle in the war of
Armageddon, is not *the* battle of Armageddon. More blood
must flow, else the "beast" from Rome shall rule the earth!
For after the overthrow of Gog, "king of the north," will not
"all the world wonder after the beast"? With "the king of
the south" and all the other Mediterranean powers now in his
league and under his banners, and, with "the king of the north"
and all his allied legions utterly destroyed, will not the cry ring
around the earth: *"Who is like unto the beast? who is able
to make war with him?"* (Rev. 13:3, 4).

"And power was given him over all kindreds, and tongues,
and nations" (v. 7).

The Roman Cæsar Deifies Himself.

World conquerors ever have been prone to deify themselves. The last Roman Cæsar will be no exception to the rule. When once our schools shall have thought to relegate the Bible to the realm of myths, and shall have eradicated the idea of a supernatural God from the minds of the masses of humanity, man, who instinctively worships, will turn to the worship of the highest power he knows—*man!* The highest power of which the natural man will have knowledge will be the conqueror of the earth—Satan's supreme manifestation in the flesh —*Antichrist!* And this spirit to deify man is already manifest in these last days as totalitarianism grows apace.

When the Roman Cæsar shall fulfill the Scriptures concerning himself, and shall "magnify himself above every god, and shall speak marvellous things against the God of gods" (Dan. 11:36)—when "he openeth his mouth in blasphemy against God, to blaspheme His name, and His tabernacle, and them that dwell in heaven" (Rev. 13:6), then shall there be erected for worship the image of himself, even as these totalitarian gods of earth have ever done, and the Scripture will be fulfilled even as it is written: "There [shall] come . . . that man of sin . . . who opposeth and exalteth himself above all that is called God or that is worshipped; so that he as God sitteth in the temple of God, shewing himself that he is God" (II Thess. 2:3, 4).

The Master solemnly warned His earthly brethren against that day:

> "When ye therefore shall see the abomination of desolation, spoken of by Daniel the prophet, stand in the holy place, (whoso readeth, let him understand:) Then let them which be in Judea flee into the mountains: . . . And except those days should be shortened, there should no flesh be saved: but for the elect's sake those days shall be shortened" (Matt. 24:15, 16, 22).

It must be borne in mind that during this earthly glorification of the Antichrist, the born-again saints of God will be safely hidden away from satanic wrath in the mansion-chambers above.

The Antichrist and the Jews.

It must also be borne in mind that when the Antichrist first comes on the scene, he is going to pose as a friend of the Jews. No Adolf Hitler can ever arise to the exalted position of the Antichrist, for Jesus said to the Jews: "I am come in My Father's name, and ye receive Me not: if another shall come in his own name, *him will ye receive*" (John 5:43). Can we conceive that the Jews would ever hail Adolf Hitler as their Savior? Impossible! A Jew would have to be a renegade, indeed, to enable him to stoop so low as to make a god out of an immoral wretch that has sunken to the depths of all that is loathsome, as has the Nazi chieftain.

Nebuchadnezzar is the pattern of the Antichrist. When the Jews came under his power, he befriended them, set them at his own table, and placed them over the affairs of his kingdom. But when the day came that he set up his image for them to worship, there is another story to tell!

Even so, when the "image of the beast" (Rev. 13:14) shall have been set up for worship in the reconstructed temple in Jerusalem, then will the eyes of the Jews be opened to the awful mistake they will have made, and they will discover the true nature of the Antichrist. Whatever else the modern Jew may be, he is not an idolater. Centuries ago he learned his lesson at a terrible price.

With the setting up of "the image of the beast," the spirit of Shadrach, Meshach, and Abednego will have returned to earth. The Jews will rebel against the decree of the Antichrist, aimed, doubtlessly, to unify all the religions of the earth—the decree that all men must worship the image of the beast, and "that as many as would not worship the image of the beast should be killed" (Rev. 13:15).

When the new Roman Cæsar, the world's last Nebuchadnezzar, shall hear that the Jews in Jerusalem refuse to bow the knee to worship his image, then all Israel will know the full meaning of the "great tribulation" foretold by the Messiah that they once rejected. As Nebuchadnezzar *"commanded that they should heat the furnace one seven times more than it was wont to be heated"* (Dan. 3:19) and cast the Jews into it, so all Israel, in the latter part of the reign of the Antichrist shall see "great tribulation, such as was not since the beginning of the world to this time, no, nor ever shall be" (Matt. 24:21). Then anti-Semitism, now spreading over the face of all the earth, shall have reached its utmost possible ferocity.

Oh, that all Israel might know the heavenly hiding place that their Messiah has gone to prepare against that day! Not knowing it, the next best they can do is to accept the "two wings of a great eagle, . . . [and] fly into the wilderness" (Rev. 12: 14). *"Then"* let them which be in Judea flee into the mountains" (Matt. 24:16).

The Cause of "The Battle of Armageddon."

By "the battle of Armageddon" we refer to the last battle of "the war of Armageddon." The cause of that "battle" is distinctly stated by the prophet Joel:

> "For, behold, in those days, and in that time, when I shall bring again the captivity of Judah and Jerusalem, I will also gather all nations, and will bring them down into the valley of Jehoshaphat, and *will plead with them there for My people and for My heritage Israel,* whom they have scattered among the nations, and parted My land. And they have cast lots for My people; and have given a boy for an harlot, and sold a girl for wine, that they might drink" (Joel 3:1-3).

This Scripture cannot be mistaken! Is it possible that any professed Christian, knowing the Scriptures, can have any part in the present-day anti-Semitic world-wide movement that is leading the world on to Armageddon? God forbid! The blindness of Israel—the stiffneckedness of Israel—the anti-Christ spirit so manifest in Israel—may richly merit chastisement. But let no Christian ever think himself to be the rod of punishment.

"The Battle of Armageddon"—Gentile Against Jew.

Contrary to popular opinion, "the battle of Armageddon" is not a battle of Gentile against Gentile but a battle in which all the nations of the earth will go forward to carry out a program which is even now the program of the German Fuehrer —*the extermination of the Jew!*

There are those who scoff at the possibility of such a "battle"! They sneer that Gentile against Jew would not make a good fight!

But it is so written! The immutable Word of God that cannot be broken declares it:

"BEHOLD . . . I will gather *all nations against Jerusalem* to battle" (Zech. 14:1, 2).

"BEHOLD, in those days, and in that time, when I shall bring again the captivity of Judah and Jerusalem, I will also gather *all nations,* and will bring them down into the valley of Jehoshaphat, and will plead with them there for My people and for My heritage Israel, whom they have scattered among the nations, and parted My land" (Joel 3:1, 2).

"BEHOLD, . . . all the people [Gentiles] . . . shall be in the seige both *against Judah and Jerusalem.* And in that day will I make Jerusalem a burdensome stone for all people . . . though *all the people of the earth be gathered together against it"* (Zech. 12:2, 3).

"BEHOLD a white horse [and on that horse, *a Jew*]. . . . And I saw the beast, and the kings of the earth, and their armies, gathered together to make war against Him that sat on the horse, and against His army" (Rev. 19:11, 19).

It is always so in the sure word of prophecy—*all nations against Jerusalem—Gentile against Jew!*

And "that will not make a good fight," you say?
We shall see!

XV

ARMAGEDDON AND—THE VICTORY!

"The Prince of This World Cometh" (John 14:30).

WHEN "the prince of this world," even Satan, shall have, in the Antichrist, his revelation in the flesh; and when, a little later, he shall come to the pinnacle of his power, then "he shall plant the tabernacles of his palace between the seas in the glorious holy mountain" (Dan. 11:45). Satan, already having imitated the Christ by riding forth on a white horse, "conquering and to conquer," will plant his palace on the sacred ground whereon our Lord "will build again the tabernacle of David which is fallen down" (Acts 15:16). In other words, Satan's man would beat the Son of David to the throne promised to Mary for her Son by the angel Gabriel:

> "And the angel said unto her, Fear not, Mary: for thou hast found favour with God. And, behold, thou shalt conceive in thy womb, and bring forth a son, and shalt call His name JESUS. He shall be great, and shall be called the Son of the Highest: and the Lord God shall give unto Him the throne of His father David: And He shall reign over the house of Jacob for ever; and of His kingdom there shall be no end" (Luke 1:30-33).

The false Messiah not only will plant his palace on "the glorious holy mountain," but he will enter the temple of God, where "in the midst of the week [of years], he shall cause the sacrifice and the oblation to cease" (Dan. 9:27); and, on the site of the altar, he shall set up his own image (Rev. 13:14-18), even "the abomination of desolation, spoken by Daniel the prophet" (Matt. 25:15, Cf. Dan. 11:27), "shewing himself that he is God" (II Thess. 2:4). Then, as we have before seen, the deluded Jews will discover that "the beast" is truly a beast, and not their Messiah. As in Babylon of old, they will refuse to worship that "abomination," and the mass of them will instinctively rush for the refuge provided for them in the wilderness (Matt. 25:16; Rev. 12:14).

A courageous remnant, however, will refuse to surrender the hallowed ground and will barricade themselves in the holy city, ready to die, if need be, but never to worship the "abomination" of hell.

Once again, the mighty Gentile antagonist of Him Who is both the Son of David and the Son of God "shall go forth with great fury to destroy"—this time, and for the last time, against the rebellious Jews. To destroy them then, he knows, would be to destroy the last vestige of rebellion against his absolute rule over the whole earth.

No wonder Jehovah loves the Jews! Time and time again, through ages past, they have breasted all the fiery darts of the devil, they have faced all the furious legions of hell, and they have endured all the agonizing tortures of the damned, that faith in the living God might not perish from the earth! It is not hard to understand why, in spite of their failure to see in Jesus Christ the Son of God their Messiah, in a day when their minds were darkened, and in spite of their temporary falling away from the pathways of their fathers of old, that God should have caused His prophet to warn the Gentile world by saying to the Jews, "He that toucheth you toucheth the apple of His eye" (Zech. 2:8.). God knows that the wandering Jew will some day return to His breast. He knows that the wandering Gentile will never return. (*Cf.* Jer. 30:10).

"The Siege of Judah and Jerusalem."

The Antichrist, Satan incarnate, once again will put the bugle to his lips, and sound his battle-cry. Those who will answer that call will come forth out of *all* the nations—*an international army,* under the command of this last captain of the devil's hosts. In that army *"all nations"* will march "against Jerusalem to battle" (Zech. 14:1). This army will be panoplied with all the latest paraphernalia of war. On they will roll and fly and march—tanks and planes and men—to the walls of Jerusalem—on for the subjugation, yea, for what they hope to be the final destruction of the Jews.

Israel, agonizer of the centuries, will writhe in the last awful spasms of agony he shall ever know. "The city shall be taken, and the houses rifled, and the women ravished"; but the armed power of all that terrible army of "all nations" shall succeed only in bringing "half of the city . . . into captivity" (Zech. 14:2). Humanly, it seems as if the handful of Jews within the holy city would be annihilated within a few short seconds by the thundering tanks and roaring planes and bursting bombs of death! But not so! There will be some very good reasons!

In the first place, the God of Israel promised that when that awful travail shall come to Israel, Israel "shall be saved out of it" (Jer. 30:7. *Cf.* Dan. 12:1). And God's promises never fail!

In the second place, Jehovah of hosts, has said:

> "Behold, I will make Jerusalem a cup of trembling unto all the people round about, when they shall be in the siege both against Judah and against Jerusalem. And in that day will I make Jerusalem a burdensome stone for all people: all that burden themselves with it shall be cut in pieces, though all the people of the earth be gathered together against it" (Zech. 12:2, 3).

In the third place, the miracle-working God has declared:

> "In that day . . . I will smite every horse with astonishment, and his rider with madness: and I will open Mine eyes upon the house of Judah, and will smite every horse of the people with blindness" (Zech. 12:4).

Insanity will grip the Gentile warriors, and they shall slay each other until the gush of blood shall reach the horse bridles (Rev. 14:20).

In the fourth place, the God of battles has revealed that

> "In that day shall the Lord defend the inhabitants of Jerusalem; and he that is feeble among them at that day shall be as David" (Zech. 12:8).

Now, if any one would know the exact meaning of that significant expression, *"shall be as David,"* if he will call up from

the shades a fellow by the name of Goliath, that once armored
giant may be able to throw some very interesting light upon
the implication of the prophetic reference to David!

In the fifth place, it is written:

> *"Then shall the Lord go forth, and fight against those
> nations, as when He fought in the day of battle"* (Zech.
> 14:3), crying:

"The day of vengeance is in Mine heart, and the year
of My redeemed is come" (Isa. 63:4). Though Satan's
"man of sin" should muster a thousand times ten thousand
German armies, they would all be ground to powder when
the "Stone of Israel" falls upon the Gentile colossi in
that day. (*Cf.* Gen. 49:23; Dan. 2:44, 45).

Would you see Him, "glorious in His apparel, travelling in
the greatness of His strength . . . mighty to save?" (Isa. 63:1).
Go stand beside the Seer of Patmos and behold that stupendous
scene! Never before and never thereafter will there be a scene
like unto it in its intensity, in its magnitude, in its grandeur,
in its terrific terribleness, in the infinity of its results:

"And I saw heaven opened, and behold a white horse;
and He that sat upon him was called Faithful and True,
and in righteousness He doth judge and make war.

"His eyes were as a flame of fire, and on His head were
many crowns; and He had a name written, that no man
knew, but He Himself.

"And He was clothed with a vesture dipped in blood:
and His name is called The Word of God.

"And the armies which were in heaven followed Him
upon white horses, clothed in fine linen, white and clean.

"And out of His mouth goeth a sharp sword, that with
it He should smite the nations: and He shall rule them
with a rod of iron: and He treadeth the winepress of the
fierceness and wrath of Almighty God.

"And He hath on His vesture and on His thigh a name
written, KING OF KINGS, AND LORD OF LORDS.

"And I saw an angel standing in the sun; and he cried
with a loud voice, saying to all the fowls that fly in the

midst of heaven, Come and gather yourselves together unto the supper of the great God;

"That ye may eat the flesh of kings, and the flesh of captains, and the flesh of mighty men, and the flesh of horses, and of them that sit on them, and the flesh of all men, both free and bond, both small and great.

"And I saw the beast, and the kings of the earth, and their armies, gathered together to make war against Him that sat on the horse, and against His army.

"And the beast was taken, and with him the false prophet that wrought miracles before him, with which he deceived them that had received the mark of the beast, and them that worshipped his image. These both were cast alive into a lake of fire burning with brimstone.

"And the remnant were slain with the sword of Him that sat upon the horse, which sword proceeded out of His mouth: and all the fowls were filled with their flesh.

"And I saw an angel come down from heaven, having the key of the bottomless pit and a great chain in his hand.

"And he laid hold on the dragon, that old serpent, which is the Devil, and Satan, and bound him a thousand years,

"And cast him into the bottomless pit, and shut him up, and set a seal upon him, that he should deceive the nations no more, till the thousand years should be fulfilled" (Rev. 19:11-20:3).

Can we add or take away a single word from that awe-inspiring, yet glorious spectacle? Needless to say that when the smoke of that battle rolls off the field, and the fowls of the air have cleared away the noisome carcasses of the challengers of the Lord of glory, then "shall the Sun of righteousness arise" over the earth "with healing in His wings" (Mal. 4:2); "and, the ransomed of the Lord shall return, and come to Zion with songs and everlasting joy upon their heads: they shall obtain joy and gladness, and sorrow and sighing shall flee away" (Isa. 35:10.) Hallelujah! Amen!